Lent,

Thanks for the support!

CHANNELING JERRY

Hope you enjoy this book.

Channel on ⚡⚡

~ Nick

CHANNELING JERRY

HOW THE MUSIC PLAYS HIS FANS

Interviews with artists influenced by Jerry Garcia and the Grateful Dead

NICK HUTCHINSON

Foreword by Dennis McNally
(Jerry Garcia. Cal Expo. Sacramento, 1991. Photo by Susana Millman.)

FOREWORD

Jerry almost never repeated himself in the course of our fairly lengthy conversations, but there was one thing: He kicked himself more than once for his lack of formal training in music. After a brief lesson on tuning from his cousin Danny, he'd said, "Let's jam," and away they went—everything else he learned he picked up by himself or from his bandmates. The end result was that his guitar playing went in all the directions his ears had gone . . . and that covers a lot of musical ground.

I bring this up because I think that this, along with his personality, is the reason so many young guitarists want to study him. He was exceedingly bright and extremely learned in music (he'd laugh to hear me say that, but it's true). But because he had never learned the "right way," he had no limits. Which meant that he could combine bluegrass and John Coltrane and have it come out Jerry Garcia. Over the course of all those shows, he shook the snow globe of music so many times and came up with so many different ways of solving musical puzzles, that he laid a trail of almost infinite possibilities. So of course people want to study the trail for clues.

There's also the personality. In the end, the music you make is who you are - certainly if you play improvisationally—and Jerry had a huge persona that was grounded in a genuine curiosity about other people, which automatically implies a certain appropriate humility. He didn't think he had all the answers, and wondered if you—any of you, even the least likely among us—might be able to teach him something. Which is why he'd ask Steve Parish to "go find me somebody weird" when he was sitting and warming up with hours to go until showtime at the Keystone Berkeley. He wasn't amusing himself with some of the street people Steve would find; he actually wanted to know their story.

One of the wiser things I ever heard was the remark by Marshall McLuhan that "If you want to be interesting, be interested." Jerry embodied that, because of course from the time he was 18 if not before, a whole bunch of people took one look at him and decided life would be more fun if they followed him around. In fancier neighborhoods, it's called charisma, and it was certainly true of him. He was interested, so everybody got interested in him.

But then, you all may have noticed that already!

So as the Warlocks and then the Grateful Dead evolved, they naturally chose improvisation as the magic key that would let them follow this open path. It was fundamental to Jerry, synchronous with his entire point of view. And the other "elder" in the band—when they began, Jerry was 23, Phil 25, Bobby 18, Bill 19, Pigpen 20—Phil, was a jazz veteran and a serious student of John Coltrane. Throw in their psychedelic initiation in the Acid Tests and improvisation was the only possible avenue for them. It would allow them to fuse their vastly different musical backgrounds into something truly unique, an American string band music that, with Robert Hunter's and later John Barlow's lyrics, became a genre unto itself.

Which was the discovery Dead Heads made around the time of the Fare Thee Well concerts in 2015. "Hey, if the band is going to stop touring, it doesn't matter so very much, because we're fans of the music, not just the band." And out of that realization has come dozens, hundreds of bands playing Dead music, each in their own way. Dead & Co. maintains its own lineage, JRAD and DSO chart different courses. It's all a matter of taste.

The end result, as Nick's conversations with these various players reveals, is that the music has such breadth and depth that every musician can find him- or herself in it. Open. Room to explore. Just the way Jerry would want it, actually.

— Dennis McNally
San Francisco, CA
May, 2020

Contents/Interviews

David Gans   5

Mark Karan   13

Garrett Deloian   21

Joni Bottari   29

Andrea Whitt   37

Vic DeRobertis   43

Katie Skene   51

John Kadlecik   59

Halina Janusz   67

Steve Kimock   73

Set Break   79

Lisa Malsberger   85

Jeff Mattson   91

Stephen Inglis   97

Anela Lauren   103

Tyler Grant   109

Joe Craven   115

Marcus Rezak   121

Joe Marcinek   125

Adam Perry   129

Josh Olken   133

(Jerry Garcia. January 1993. Oakland, CA. Photo by Susana Millman.)

PREFACE

Of all the uniquely talented musicians in the Grateful Dead, perhaps one stood out the most: Jerome John Garcia – or simply "Jerry," as he came to be known. Ever since the first notes drifted from his amp, other players have felt the pull of his artistic expression and since then many have attempted to capture the essence of his sound . . . or to "channel Jerry" if you will.

Is this ongoing devotion to Garcia about replicating the exact sounds that he made? Or is it an attempt to connect with the spirit that teased those notes out and to relate to the unseen impulse that first drove the San Francisco Bay Area teen to broadcast his angst and creativity via the strings of a musical instrument?

Through a series of interviews with some of the artists who have found themselves standing in Garcia's figurative shoes since his passing in 1995, and others who have simply appreciated Jerry's style and put their own spin on it, I attempt to shed a little light on his enduring popularity.

Channeling Jerry is partly about Jerry Garcia and the Grateful Dead, but it's more about the variety of musicians who are influenced by Garcia's artistry and those who absorb and regenerate it.

By no means do these pages attempt to include all of the Jerry-inspired players in the extended Grateful Dead music community. Most Deadheads have a favorite Jerry practitioner or two, or three. Accomplished Garcia devotees are many and varied and Jerry's influence is diverse and wide.

Like a rose unfolding or a universe being born, his energy still crackles. From the more precise and convincing replicators to the looser interpreters of Jerry's vibe as well as a few non-lead guitar playing musicians, these chapters attempt to gain a current impression of Garcia's legacy. *Channeling Jerry* is dedicated to all the musicians and fans around the globe who endeavor to keep the flame burning. – N. Hutchinson.

Jerome J. Garcia
Born Aug. 1, 1942. San Francisco, CA.
Died Aug. 9, 1995. Forest Knolls, CA.

ACKNOWLEDGEMENTS

I am indebted to my wife, Keller, who helped me develop the idea for this book. I extend profound thanks to Grateful Dead historian and publicist Dennis McNally, who acted as an advisor and contributor to the project; and David Gans, who also provided valuable input and support. I'm grateful for all the talented and thoughtful musicians who agreed to be interviewed. I'd like to acknowledge the members of Jerry's Middle Finger who were very supportive in the early phases of the project, including Halina Janusz who kindly helped facilitate conversations with other artists. Andrea Whitt, of the duo Katie & Andrea, was not only an interview subject but also illustrated the beautiful *Channeling Jerry* watercolor (which is featured as part of a custom jigsaw puzzle by Liberty Puzzles of Boulder, Colorado). Photographers Susana Millman, Rich Saputo, David Tracer, Hal Masonberg, Alan Hess, Matt Beauchemin, JD Cohen, Lori Pedemonti, Ali Jay, Libby Gamble, Liz Gleeson, Gwendolyn Anne Ross, Jake Cox, Tony Stack and a few others who allowed the use of their work, were invaluable. I also extend thanks to writer and longtime friend, Nick Paumgarten, for contributing his insightful words to the project. Like a Grateful Dead concert, *Channeling Jerry* is an expression of community. In loving memory of my father, Paul Hutchinson, who encouraged me to read, write and follow my muse.

(David Gans. Folsom Field. Boulder, Colorado. Dead & Co. June 2017. Photo courtesy of D. Gans.)

David Gans

David Gans is partly responsible for the resurgence of live Grateful Dead-inspired music following Jerry Garcia's death in 1995. Gans's 1997 benefit shows, with his musical collective the Broken Angels, helped rekindle bassist Phil Lesh's interest for performing in the years after Garcia played his last notes. Lesh's outings with Phil Lesh & Friends grew from the Broken Angels performances, during which the famous bassist joined Gans and company for a few sets. Since playing those gigs with Phil, Gans has continued on his own musical journey. He also continues his well-appreciated work on the airwaves, where his longtime syndicated show, The Grateful Dead Hour, broadcasts widely as does his talkshow Tales from the Golden Road, with co-host Gary Lambert, on SiriusXM Radio. Gans's contribution to the Grateful Dead community along with his passion for the music and its fanbase is enormous. In a low-key, often behind-the-scenes way, he remains one of the key figures keeping the music in the ears of a wide group of listeners.

When did you first start playing an instrument?

I started when I was a kid. My parents got me a violin. Then they took it away and gave me a clarinet. So all through grade school, junior high and high school I played the clarinet. I began playing the guitar in my teens sometime around the spring of 1969. I also started writing my own songs at the time that I picked up the guitar. I was fifteen years old and I was composing tortured teenager poems. My brother took a couple of them and turned the words into songs and taught me a few chords on his guitar. So the first thing I ever played on the guitar was my own songs. I think it's important that I began developing my own voice at the same time that I started to study other people's music. I never wanted to just play other artists' material.

Where were you living at that time?

In San Jose, California. I was born in Los Angeles but my family moved to northern California when I was twelve. I went to three different high schools in the Bay Area before I graduated from high school in San Jose in 1970. Then I goofed around at San Jose State for a couple years before dropping out and moving to Berkeley.

What exactly was it that made you want to move to Berkeley?

A woman. Also a buddy of mine who was moving back to San Jose at the same time that I was moving to Berkeley said, "Look up my friends on Etna Street." They were students at Cal, and I started playing Grateful Dead music with them. That became the beginning of a musical relationship that lasted thirty years. We loved the Dead and Commander Cody and His Lost Planet Airmen. We also loved Asleep at the Wheel. All these groups played regularly in the Bay Area at the time. We were early fans of what came to be known as Americana music. We adopted those bands' style of playing their own material as well as other people's songs and treating it all equally. One of the most important things about the Grateful Dead is that they had a huge love for other people's music and they gave it equal weight in their own performances. We took that same approach. We didn't just play stuff that we learned from the Grateful Dead, because Willie Nelson came along and Emmy Lou Harris was out there and all these other amazing country songwriters, so we adopted their tunes too.

Did your band have a name?

The band had various names. I think they were called the Bobcats when I joined them. We didn't really have an official band name until the early eighties when the rhythm guitarist, Alan Feldstein, and I started a band called the Reptiles. I met them around 1973 or 1974 when we were playing in backyards and at fraternity parties for the most part. We didn't start looking for bar gigs until the eighties.

Were you trying to launch a career as a musician?

Playing music was important to me, but in the mid-seventies I began to write about music when *BAM* (Bay Area Music) *Magazine* started here in California. Writing gave me an opportunity to meet people and learn more about music. They flew me to L.A. to interview Leo Fender and I went to Michigan to interview Joe Walsh. I wound up spending ten years working for music and recording industry magazines. I also worked as the music editor of *Mix Magazine* and I was a senior editor at *Record Magazine* for most of its existence. I got an immense education from my time as a journalist and I got to sit down, twice, with artists such as Randy Newman and I interviewed [legendary record producer] Ted Templeman. And I got to interview Jerry Garcia and Bob Weir. So journalism was a really great way to enrich myself. Then in the mid-nineties I recorded an album with a buddy of mine because we wanted the life experience of making a record and right around that time I got a call to play at an event in New York. After Jerry died I thought the Grateful Dead thing was going to wind down and that I should get back to doing my own music or I was going to have to get a regular job. But it turned out that this whole batch of Deadhead-like music festivals sprang up in the wake of the Grateful Dead stopping and I got invitations to go and play at some of them. So I started touring after Jerry died beginning around 1997 and I did my first tour as a solo artist in 1998. I was late getting started as a national stage musician but that means that I was able to do it as a sane adult instead of as a self-destructive kid.

Can you share a bit about how Phil Lesh came to sit in with your band the Broken Angels in 1997?

A guy named Dan McGonagle was doing Grateful Dead deejay shows in bars around the Bay Area and he approached me in 1997 and wanted to do a thing at a bar near the University of California campus called Larry Blake's. He called it The Dead Experiment. He wanted me to put a live band together and play a set and then he would do his deejay thing until closing. So I got the idea to start what I called the Broken Angels, where I'd put together a different band every week. It was really really fun to do. We'd play a set and then Dan would do his Dead deejay portion of the night. We had that gig for about six months or so and then basically we got fired because all our fans were potheads and they didn't drink enough beer, but I liked it and so I started playing at a placed called the Ashkenaz.

The Ashkenaz is a great music and dance club in Berkeley that was founded in 1973. It was owned by a guy named David Nadel. Well one night David kicked this guy out of the club for being drunk and the guy came back and shot David. This was in 1996. David died a few days later. He was such a wonderful and generous person and after he died the community went to his family and made an arrangement to buy the club from them and run it as a non-profit. I was part of the group that organized that effort and I served on the board of that non-profit for a couple years. Another friend of mine, Gordon Taylor, had this idea that we could produce a benefit concert and buy a sound system for the club from Meyer Sound which makes great sound systems. I went to Helen Meyer and asked her if they'd be willing to give us a deal on some of their speakers and accept the proceeds from some benefit concerts as kind of a payment plan. They gave us half-off on the speakers and agreed to take whatever we earned from the benefit concerts until it was paid off. This was September of 1997. My concept for the Broken Angels was that we'd get a whole bunch of Dead-loving musicians together and do some all-star gigs. At the time Phil and Jill Lesh were starting the Unbroken Chain Foundation and my wife and I were on their board. They were planning the first of their events which came to be known as the *PhilHarmonia*, which occurred in December of 1997. I was working with Phil on that event and planning my benefit shows at the same time and I said to Phil one day "Hey we're gonna be doing this thing and it would make a gigantic difference if you would come and play a couple songs with us. It would just blow every-one's minds and help us sell out." He didn't agree at first but he decided to do it at the last minute. When we told everyone he was going to play it was standing-room only.

So Phil got onstage with us and we did "Scarlet Begonias" into "New Speedway Boogie" with him on bass. It was a wonderful experience and he had a great time doing it. I remember standing with him at the back of the dance floor with my wife and he looked out at the room and said, "Oh my god this amazing. This music is like a language that people speak." And I was like, "FUCK YEAH! Multiply this by about ten thousand and you'll have a sense of how we felt standing in the audience when you were playing!"

So he liked the idea and we did several more benefit shows. We played at the Maritime Hall and did another one at the Fillmore. This was November and December of 1997 and January of 1998. We did three benefits for The Unbroken Chain Foundation with the Broken Angels and Phil was a special guest for part of that. As you can imagine it was one of the highlights of my life. I was mind-blown to be part of it. Phil got the idea and then he started doing Phil Lesh & Friends after that and Bob's your uncle.

What Kind of guitars do you like to play?

For acoustic, I own a Martin D-35 that I bought new in 1973. And I have two acoustic guitars that were made for me by a luthier in the Bay Area named Mario DeSio. I also have a 1956 Les Paul Junior, and I have a Rick Turner model 1 electric that I bought from him in 1981. My primary travel instrument is a Rick Turner Renaissance RS6 and the thing about that guitar is that it's one of those stage acoustics that's got a sealed chamber, so you plug it in and it sounds like an acoustic guitar, but it also has an electric pickup which sounds like an electric guitar if you plug it into an amp. It's a good stage guitar because I can only carry one instrument on the road and it's the perfect hybrid. I can play a solo gig with it and it sounds like a big fat acoustic guitar but when I'm onstage with a band I play it through my pedals and it sounds like a great electric guitar. So it's one guitar that does everything I need it to do. I don't geek out on instruments. I think because I started as a songwriter, I've never fetishized them. To me they're tools to help me tell my story. It's never been about the guitar itself to me and I've never been a fiend about having a tone that has to be exactly so. As a practical matter when I'm out on the road and I'm at the mercy of whatever sounds system I have to plug into, or I'm at a festival where I have five minutes to set my shit up and soundcheck, I can't afford to be that picky. You can't be that picky or you're just going to have an unhappy time of it. As long as my stuff works I'm happy. I'm not all precious about having to sound perfect. I have a great guitar that always sounds good. Sound people will actually come up to me after a gig and say, "Jesus that thing sounds great." If you get the right tools you don't have to sweat the specifics of whether your overdrive is set just so.

What was it about Jerry and the music of the Grateful Dead that caught your ear?

I was living with a guy, a classmate of mine from high school, who I was writing songs with. He had been bugging me to go see the Dead for months. I didn't think I was going to like them because their music was kind of out there and loud and stuff. I had no idea how sophisticated it was. So finally, he talked me into going. We took heroic doses of LSD and went to Winterland and I was way out of my head, but these little bits of things etched themselves in my mind and stuck with me and when I got back home I started listening to their records and I figured out what it was that I'd heard. One of the songs that had grabbed me, from the album *Ace,* was "Greatest Story Ever Told," which to me is the quintessential Bob Weir guitar song. All the amazing things about Bobby's style are in that song if you listen to it. So their songs appealed to me first. They were a lot more interesting than a lot of the pop music I was listening to. I was a big fan of Crosby, Stills and Nash, Jackson Browne, The Eagles, Cat Stevens, Elton John, . . . all the singer-songwriter type stuff of the early seventies. But the Grateful Dead had all this other stuff going on. Their songs didn't tell you everything they know right away. They kind of insinuated and left a lot of room for you to think along with them. That was a way of songwriting that I thought was sustainable and attractive.

It made me realize that songs could be more literary and not just silly little ditties that are designed to sell a million copies. Their music intrigued me and made me realize that I could write with

(David Gans realizing what music can do.
Photo courtesy of D. Gans.)

more depth and more sophistication and they inspired me to create more of my own stuff. When I started to learn about what was going on with the jams I realized that this music was a whole language of its own and that their shows were a conversation between the players. That's when I started looking for people to jam with and with whom I could have conversations like that. I learned that a show was a dialogue between the musicians and the audience. It wasn't just to stand up there and play the same thing every time. It was a living, breathing thing. Everything about the Grateful Dead opened up my sense of what music is and what it can do.

Is there anything about Dead cover bands that makes you go hmmm?

Well, our rule would be let's play "Scarlet Begonias" into ANYTHING BUT "Fire on the Mountain." Let's not play the same combinations the Dead played. Let's mix it up and play different things. And let's combine it with our music, which is exactly what the Dead were doing. To me they were a catalyst of creativity and something to emulate but not something to copy. It drives me nuts when people mindlessly copy. The last thing I ever want to do is to stand up on stage and pretend to be Jerry. Why do that? Jerry's singing voice was higher than most people's singing voices, so we have this phenomenon of guys who are playing guitars shaped like Jerry's guitar, imitating Jerry

Garcia's style of guitar playing and trying to sing in a voice like Jerry's in notes that aren't available to them because they don't have Jerry Garcia's voice box. These bands insist on playing exactly like the Dead even though they might not have the proper skills or the proper physical requirements. That doesn't interest me. I want to have the conversation in my own voice.

How do you feel about the proliferation of Dead bands in general?

People love the music and so they take these songs and they sing them. It's the folk process. When I was doing the Broken Angels gigs with Phil I got an email from a guy that basically said, "How dare you sing 'Stella Blue.' That song should have died with Jerry." Well how wrong could you be?! You think Jerry wanted the song to die with him?! These songs were meant to be sung by people. Blair Jackson and I interviewed Jerry in 1981 and I said to Jerry in that conversation, "This music is going to outlive the guys who made it." And Jerry said, "Yeah that's how we feel about it too." The fact that there are hundreds of bands around the country playing Grateful Dead music is a wonderful thing. These songs are going to keep living because so many people love them and want to play them. I perform with a Hawaiian slack key guitarist [Stephen Inglis] and a harpist [Anela Lauren] in a band we call Fragile Thunder. It's a whole new approach to Grateful Dead music. And there's a band here in Northern California called Wake the Dead, which is comprised of accomplished Celtic musicians who play the music of the Dead in a Celtic style and who mix it up with jigs and reels. And there's an all-female Grateful Dead band from Florida called Brown Eyed Women. It's great that everyone is playing this music. The songs are eventually going to become part of the folk canon and no one will even care that they're Grateful Dead songs. They're just great songs.

Which is where Jerry picked it up to begin with right? He was covering the folk canon and interpreting his favorite songs . . .

Exactly. We're all continuing the same tradition. I consider myself a son of the Grateful Dead because I'm doing exactly what they did. I'm writing music. I'm interpreting music. I'm improvising music and I'm offering an honest, real-time experience that is unique to me, which is what they did. But I'm also bringing other stuff to it, just as they did. The last thing I want to do is imitate anyone else. I'm inspired by them to make my own music.

Do you think the music has evolved at all since Jerry died?

We have a huge range of interpretations for sure. Dark Star Orchestra is like the Grateful Dead wax museum. They replicate the vibe of a Dead show. They replicate the hardware and everything else and they're doing a magnificent job of it. In a way I think this frees up the rest of us. And it frees up the remaining Dead band members too. Bob Weir doesn't have to recapture what he once did because Rob Eaton is doing that. So Bob can play the way Bob plays now. The remaining band members are moving ahead with their projects. Dead & Company is kind of a Dead cover band but they're doing it with amazing players. They're taking the material and carrying it forward. I love a "Dark Star" from Dead & Company almost as much as I love a "Dark Star" by the Grateful Dead because Dead & Company plays it brilliantly. So the fact that there are all these people moving the music forward is fantastic. Look what JRAD (Joe Russo's Almost Dead) is doing. It's a super high-energy Grateful Dead thing that's evolving the music. We have a bunch of younger bands bringing energy to this music. There's Grateful Shred and Jerry's Middle Finger who are making a lot of noise. Next month I'm playing with a band in Dayton, Ohio, called Great Northern String Band and they're just a really sweet, seven-piece acoustic band that plays Grateful Dead and Jerry Garcia Band music their own way. All of this stuff is an indication that I was right thirty years ago when I said to Jerry, "This music is going to outlive you." It's doing so, and it's wonderful.

(Mark Karan. 2014. Photo by Anne Cutler.)

Mark Karan

M ark Karan was introduced to fans of the Grateful Dead through his work in bands including The Other Ones, RatDog & Bob Weir, Planet Drum with Mickey Hart, and Phil & Friends. Over the course of his accomplished career he has logged time in the studios of Los Angeles, where he recorded with musicians such as Huey Lewis, Paul Carrack, Dave Mason, Delaney Bramlett and Jesse Colin Young, among others. Karan, who also fields his own band, Jemimah Puddleduck, is an inventive lead guitarist whose style includes elements of soul, pop, blues, psychedelic and jam. He has also toured with the groups Terrapin Flyer (featuring Melvin Seals) and LIVE DEAD '69. He continues to perform with a variety of musicians from the extended Grateful Dead music community and beyond.

Did you grow up in a musical household or did you break the mold?

Well it kind of depends on whether you're talking nature or nurture. My birth father was a jazz trumpet player, though I never saw him past the age of two. So I didn't have a lot of music around the house in terms of people playing music or being musicians but there's something in the genetics for sure. I grew up in a musical household in that there was a lot of music being listened to.

How old were you when you first picked up the guitar?

I was about eight or nine. When I first started it was about folk music for me. My parents bought me a horrible first guitar and I tried to learn how to play on it. I was also in the San Francisco Boys Choir and we used to go to music camp every summer where I met a guy who was kind of a prototype hippie. It was 1963 or so and he was already sporting a ponytail. He was a folk singer and a guitar player and I was fascinated and we took a liking to each other and I started learning guitar from him.

I remember you telling me you were in a group called the Joyful Watermelon early on in your career?

That was my first gigging band. It was formed around the Haight scene, as you can probably tell from the name. Before that I was in a few mid-sixties garage bands, including one called Linear Motion and another that was called the Mass Media.

When you were playing with your early bands were you a fan of Dead music and/or a Deadhead?

Well, there was no such thing as Deadheads at the time. There were people who hung out in the Haight and who were influenced by the music coming out of the scene there and the Grateful Dead was one of the bands. My friends and I definitely liked the Dead and all of those bands and I went to a lot of Grateful Dead shows. We would go to Winterland or the Fillmore or Golden Gate Park or wherever, and if the Dead were part of it that was awesome. We loved them but I was also way into Quicksilver Messenger Service and The sons of Champlin and The Jefferson Airplane. And there were also a lot of lesser-known bands around that scene that I really enjoyed. The Deadhead thing didn't happen until later. When I was in high school, which is a little later than what we're talking about, my friends and I used to follow the Sons of Champlin in much the same way that the Deadheads wound up following the Dead.

Do you remember where your first Grateful Dead show was?

I think it was my birthday weekend when I turned eleven, which would have been in 1966 at the Fillmore.

Do you you have any special memories from that time?

It's possible that I saw Jerry wandering around the Haight, but I don't remember it specifically. At that point they weren't really stars, they were just people. You would see musicians wandering around. I'm not great at remembering specific stories in that sense. Kind of like when I was out touring with RatDog . . . it all blends together unless something triggers an exact memory.

Was there an aha moment for you in terms of wanting to play in the vein of the Dead?

Well I've always liked playing Grateful Dead songs, but I've never been a guy who likes to just play in the style of something. I like hearing the guys from the Grateful Dead play the Grateful Dead and if they're playing with current-time players then I think it's awesome that those players are playing with guys from the Grateful Dead to honor the style. But I'm not that thrilled with the proliferation of cover bands that are trying to ape what already has come and gone. I think Jerry probably would have appreciated people continuing to grow and explore and taking what they did as a jumping-off point.

Was there ever anything about the Dead's music that you didn't like?

Oh hell no, they were a band that we loved, but, like I said, they were just one of a bunch of bands that I liked. The whole San Francisco scene was very alive and there was a huge amount of creativity flying around. There were lots of incredible bands and new styles and approaches to making music. The Dead really didn't become . . . how to put it . . . the ultimate Haight Ashbury band until much later. No one really thinks about all the great bands that were part of that scene anymore even though those bands had hit records – and yet the Grateful Dead as a phenomenon is highly influential. The huge explosion around the Dead didn't happen until "Touch of Grey" [in 1987] and by then it had been a very long time since I'd started checking them out.

Was Dead music always a part of your repertoire?

Sort of. Back in the day I played Grateful Dead songs at parties and stuff, when I was eighteen, nineteen, twenty, twenty-one or something like that. But I was also listening to a lot of r&b and shortly thereafter the whole L.A. country thing exploded and the blue-eyed soul thing exploded and people such as David Bowie were coming out and shaking up the base of rock and roll. I probably listened to the Dead and all the other bands from the psychedelic scene from about 1966 to about 1975 or 1976. I enjoyed it and then I was like, "Well I've listened to this for a long time what else is out there?" There's a lot of music in the world. One of the thing that frustrates me in the Grateful Dead scene is that many of the Deadheads who I've encountered, though not all of course, would rather see a mediocre Dead band play Grateful Dead songs rather than seeing an incredible band play songs that they've never heard before.

When you were playing with The Other Ones were you sharing the lead guitar duty with Steve Kimock the whole time?

Yeah except for one show when he didn't play, which was around 2000, for a New Year's show I think.

When you joined Phil, Bobby and "the boys" was there a feeling that you were filling in for Jerry?

Well, that wasn't what they wanted. Things have changed since that point maybe, but at that time they didn't want people who were new on the block to mimic Jerry. They were like, "Hey we want you to come in and bring YOU to the party." So I decided not to trip on it. I thought that would be an easy way to shoot oneself in the foot—to go out in front of this crowd and attempt to take the place of this beloved human being and iconic musician who they had adored for thirty-five years.

Did you study any of his chops before jumping in?

No more than just to learn the songs. I didn't go out and learn a bunch of Jerry licks so that I could sound like Jerry.

Do you think Dead music has changed much since 1995?

Well, a lot of it is not stuff I gravitate to, but I definitely appreciate the idea behind bands like Wake the Dead, which does Celtic interpretations of Grateful Dead songs. It's a new angle. There's also a band called the Grateful Bluegrass Boys who take a bluegrass approach that's for real. I like that too. I've actually done a couple shows where I've culled the blues, soul and r&b material of the Dead and interpreted it in more of an authentic blues place than a Grateful Dead-ish blues approach. I like that kind of thing because you can infuse the music with alternate sensibilities. I don't hear a lot people taking the Dead's music and seeing what's next. Even if you're talking about some of the latter-day Dead-related outfits I'm not sure they did or do anything new. It's a nice continuation of the same thing. These were and are good bands, but they don't go anywhere new. My thinking is where are the new songs? Where are the rearrangements of the older songs? Where's the new art? Where's the new growth?!

RatDog and Weir pushed the envelope a bit . . .

Definitely. Bob's sensibility was that he added jazz musicians to the mix rather than rock and psychedelic musicians. So what wound up coming out of the music, even though we were playing music that was rooted in rock, was that there were elements of jazz and other things. Some of the fans didn't really like it, because it was too sleepy for them or it was weird having harmonies where they weren't there before, but I always liked it because it was unique and different. At one point we had DJ Logic in RatDog. I mean having a deejay scratching in the context of Grateful Dead music . . . we got some flak.

(Mark Karan. Sunshine Daydream Festival. 2005. Photo courtesy of Lori Pedemonti.)

How do you feel about the fact that so many people play Dead music now?

To me it seems like a lot of focusing on what's gone before. I mean people should do what they want to do, but it's kind of weird that you can't go to a major city in this country and not encounter at least half-a-dozen steadily working Dead cover bands. It seems like overkill to me. I'm a musician by trade, but also by nature. Having come from the generation that the Grateful Dead came from, I'm a bit younger, but it was always about what's next and let's explore. If the Grateful Dead had just imitated one band that they totally loved then we would not have the Grateful Dead. They weren't just exploring one thing that came before them, they were exploring lots of things that came before them and coming up with their own unique blend of influences and what-have-you as opposed to just going, "All I listen to is the Grateful Dead and all I play are songs that the Grateful Dead played." One of the things the cracks me up is the number of times that Deadheads will say that they hate country music and then they'll request "Mama Tried" or "Big River." They're listening to Merle Haggard or Johnny Cash whether they're aware of it or not. I feel like a lot of the older Deadheads get the sense of adventure and discovery and the going for something unique, but many of the younger ones who came aboard, starting with "Touch of Grey," have resulted in new generations that don't always have a sense of the history and the roots of this thing that they love.

Can we talk a little bit about when you got on the scene with The Other Ones?

Yeah, when I first went into rehearsals for The Other Ones and we were learning material, it was pretty clear what my history was because they'd pull out "Sugar Magnolia" and I was right there. They'd pull out "The Other One" and I was right there. And they'd pull out this or that song that I had been listening to when I was listening to the Grateful Dead and I knew it. But then they'd pull out "Lost Sailor" and "Saint of Circumstance" or "Shakedown Street" or the "Terrapin Station" suite and I'd go, "What's that stuff? How's that go?!" It was new for me because I hadn't been listening to what had come out since I first started listening to the band. So there was a group of songs that I had grown up listening to the Grateful Dead doing and with which I was familiar and some newer material to which I hadn't paid as much attention.

Did that impact how you went about playing the material?

Even if I hadn't consciously thought about it, what Jerry had done with those songs was running around in my mind somewhere. Some people think I don't have any Jerry in my playing and I don't know what to say about that, but when I would play those older songs I think it was obvious that I was influenced by what he did with them the many times that I heard him play them. And some of those times that I heard them I was under the influence of psychedelics so they went deep into my brain. When we would do the newer songs that I wasn't familiar with and that I hadn't seen a bunch of times in concert, I wound up playing those more like Mark. I never studied music theory and I'm not one of those guys that tries to really play it like Jerry. But you can hear his influence in my playing when I cover the older stuff.

Do you find it interesting that Grateful Dead music has kind of become its own genre?

Well, in a way it is. It's funny because unlike most other genres it's material-specific. So like when you say "blues" you don't have to do any specific song, it's an approach to playing music. When you say Grateful Dead . . . well, for example, when I played in my band Jemimah Puddleduck I always felt that the concept of that group was very Grateful Dead. The approach was, "We're going to play these songs that are rooted in Americana, be it blues, country, folk, soul or whatever, with more or less of a jazz music format, and we're gonna play the head and then all bets are off while we go instrumental and explore and when we're done exploring, we're going to come back to the head." Well I did that with Puddleduck but I didn't do it using only Grateful Dead songs. I think that the band was a great band, and one of my favorite bands I've ever been in, but we did not get a huge amount of recognition and success even though I think we were really delivering the goods and I think that had a lot to do with the fact that we didn't play a lot of actual Grateful Dead songs.

(Mark Karan. The Mint. Los Angeles. 2013. Photo by Alan Hess.)

The Grateful Dead didn't have the market cornered on taking a musical theme and exploring it, that was part of jazz . . .

Yeah, that's sort of my point. The Grateful Dead is to my way of thinking one of the first bands to take the sensibility and concept that was associated with jazz and to apply it to rock and roll.

Do you think putting acid on top of what they were doing helped them to take that approach to exploring the music?

Yeah I do, although I don't think that's all of it either. It was a confluence of events. It was the sexual revolution and the explorational musical revolution too. There was a social revolution going on and a lot of political activity. Eastern thought and philosophy was getting looked at a lot as well. All these things sort of coalesced at a moment in time to create this thing. So yeah it had something to do with it, but also the sense of the time, the sense of newness and exploration and desire for freedom. All that stuff too.

Can you tell me a little about what gear you like to use?

I think gear is up to the individual, but I'm not a huge fan of people having guitars built that are just like Jerry's guitars or using McIntosh power amps and modified Twin Reverb amps to copy something that someone else has done. More power to them if that's what they want to do, but I'm more interested in and excited by doing something new, not just reproducing the same thing that has been around for the last fifty or sixty years. That said, I'm also a vintage freak and that includes music as well as gear. It's a funny balancing act for me because I love old music and I love new stuff that's different and explorational. Keep in mind that someone like Jeff Mattson is a Garcia guy, but he gets there in his own way. Some people buy the preamps and they use the same brand of pedals and they use the loop in the guitar and all the signature Jerry stuff and that's great if that's what they want to do, but someone like Jeff, who just loves the music, gets there however he gets there. He's not hung up on using the exact gear that Jerry used. That's kind of been my approach too. I'm inspired by people but I don't try to imitate them.

(Garrett Deloian. Skull &
Roses Music Festival. 2019.
Photo by Rich Saputo.)

Garrett Deloian

Garrett Deloian is the lead guitarist for the California-based group Jerry's Middle Finger, which pays tribute to the music and spirit of the Jerry Garcia Band. Deloian cut his teeth on blues and heavy metal before falling in love with the sound of Garcia and the Grateful Dead. His precise and energetic flourishes on the fretboard reflect his early training in those genres. Deloian brings energy, enthusiasm and skill to his Jerry-inspired work in JMF, which is one of the most convincing Garcia Band experiences in the business.

When did you start playing music and where?

I grew up in Littleton, Colorado, which is part of Denver. The first guitar I had I found in my basement when I was about eight years old. It belonged to my uncle. He'd brought it back from Vietnam but somehow it just wound up in our basement and I kind of fooled around with it until I finally got the courage up to ask my mom if I could have it. She said, "Yeah bring it upstairs, it's yours." So that's when I started playing. We had a next door neighbor who was able to show me how to tune it and I never put it down after that.

What kind of guitar was it?

I think it was an old Japanese-made guitar, could have been a Silvertone maybe or something like that. I wish I still had it.

How old were you when you started playing out?

I didn't start gigging until long after I started playing. I learned how to play pretty much on my own by listening to Beatles records and then when I got into junior high school I met some other kids who were into music and we'd get together. Some guy showed my how to play barre chords and stuff. I think I discovered the Grateful Dead when I was maybe fifteen or so, while I was working at this Italian restaurant washing dishes. One of the guys who worked there on the pizza line had a boombox with him every night and when he'd close the kitchen down he always had really good high-quality soundboard bootlegs. Every night I'd creep up there and ask him what he was listening to and he would say, "The Grateful Dead." He'd listen to something completely different every night. One night he'd be playing a 1971 show and then the next night he'd play something from 1983. It didn't make a lot of sense to me. The only record I had was *Aoxomoxoa* (1969), which I'd bought on vinyl because I thought the album cover was cool. But none of his bootlegs sounded like my album.

What other music were you into at the time?

Primarily the Beatles. And around that time I got into some heavy metal of the period, or maybe something a little earlier than that, like Black Sabbath or Ozzy's band and Iron Maiden. I was also into Americana-style music that I'd heard around my house. I had an uncle who lived with us for a while and he turned me on to all kinds of stuff.

Were you able to shred some metal licks and did you attempt to try and play in that style for a while?

Yeah. They had these cassette tapes called Hot Licks back in the day that came with a little booklet. I had one that was by Tony Iommi from Black Sabbath and it had maybe 120 different guitar licks on there from all these different songs. He'd play the lick in context so you could hear it in the song and then he'd go, "Okay here it is at normal speed." Then he'd play it again at half-speed. And there was also tablature. So I figured a bunch of those out.

Maybe playing those metal licks is analogous to Garcia's early bluegrass training . . . great for the fingers . . .

Yeah, totally.

Did you get to see the Grateful Dead play live?

I did, but it wasn't until 1990 because I was still in high school and my folks were very conservative. There was no way they were gonna let me go to Red Rocks in 1987. I was fifteen and there was no chance. The only person I knew who was a Deadhead was the guy from the restaurant where I worked and he was quite a bit older so that wasn't going to happen. Then the Dead got banned from Red Rocks in '87, so I had to wait until 1990 in Kansas. I saw them at Sandstone Amphitheater on the fourth of July and it was on from there. But I was still young and my parents were strict, so it was kind of tough to get to their concerts, though I managed to take in a pretty good handful.

Did you have a revelatory moment with the music?

Well, maybe my aha moment was putting that needle down on *Aoxomoxoa*. And it's weird because when I listened to that record for the first time I didn't have any kind of context. Like I said, I literally bought the album because of the album cover. I was going to visit Germany as part of a school trip and I bought a bunch of records and then recorded them on cassette tapes so I could listen on the tour bus and that was one of them. From when I first put the needle down I couldn't stop listening to it. It was so strange and weird and quirky that I just loved it. I don't know what it was about it and I guess from there I think it was hearing all the different bootlegs that the guy brought into the restaurant. It was like how can one band have so many different sounds and styles and tones?! Their catalog was so huge and that made it interesting to me, plus Garcia's guitar playing was just phenomenal.

And that was when you were about fifteen?

Yeah, from about fifteen and sixteen, seventeen, eighteen is when I really started learning how to play the guitar along the lines of learning Grateful Dead music. At the time my skills were so rudimentary that I really learned a lot more from Bobby's playing than from Jerry. I followed the chord progressions based on Weir's rhythm playing. I wasn't much of a lead player when I was sixteen.

Did you say you started playing in bands at some point in Denver?

Yeah, when I was in middle school I started playing in a couple little garage projects with other kids. We didn't gig much but we had some talent shows and stuff like that. We played for a couple school dances. When I turned eighteen I met some folks who knew about these blues jams around Denver and that's when I met a friend of mine, Paul Niemiec, who's still a good buddy. He's a fantastic player. So that was my first experience playing out really. It became a regular thing. I'd tag along to the blues jams with Paul and he sort of became my guitar mentor. He taught me a lot.

Was he a Deadhead?

No not at all. He's a big blues guy and jazz guy. He knew all these jazz chords and could solo through complicated changes. It just blew me away. He taught me a lot of stuff.

How'd you get involved with Jerry's Middle Finger?

That's a bit of a fast-forward, but I spent some time down in Florida for a while where I was teaching scuba and playing in some blues bands and then I wound up in Culver City as part of a business move to teach scuba in California. My friend Rodney [Newman] the drummer also lives in Culver City, so he and I reconnected musically. The two of us put together a project called the Knuckles where we recorded a whole record on which the two of us played and sang all the parts. It's out there on Spotify. But from there we had a mutual friend down in Palos Verdes who played bass. We're all Deadheads and he invited us down to play one time with a friend of his named Nick Sandoval who knew the Bobby parts real well and who plays with Stu Allen from time to time. So we went down and jammed with him and we were like "Wow this is cool. This is a lot of fun." It felt like it was really happening so we kinda just kept going with that for a little while. It was difficult to keep doing a whole Grateful Dead thing though because there are so many moving parts to that. You need two drummers, you need a Bobby and a PA system and all that. It's just kind of involved. So we pared it down and decided to play JGB-style stuff. And that's kind of how Jerry's Middle Finger evolved into what it is now.

And that's the gist of JMF right? It's pretty much a Jerry Garcia Band tribute?

Yes, it really is. That's our focus. We'll throw in a Dead cover here and there because we like doing that, but mostly we try to get as authentic a Jerry Garcia Band sound as we can with all the Motown, r&b and blues that infuses JGB sets.

As a guitar player who appreciates metal and blues and other genres, what about Jerry's style do you like?

There's so much. There are so many things about his playing that are just fascinating. One of those things is that tone. That sound is unique. When you hear Garcia you know it's him. His tone always captured my ear. It's like, "Wow what's that little extra magic thing you've got in there?!" As far as his playing is concerned I try and get it right; and to try and nail Jerry is really hard. Because you have to really concentrate on what you're playing and how you're phrasing it. He had all these little signature things that he did, such as the way he uses triplets and the way he did the fanning technique with his right hand on the crescendos and things. I call that the humming bird. His use of scales is magnificent. I have two other musical loves. I spend a lot of time listening to classical music and I spend a lot of time listening to classical Indian music. One of the things that I think people miss a lot with Jerry's playing is the way he uses bends. He bends notes in really subtle ways. A lot of times he'll play a note and then play one half-step below the note and then bend back up into the note. He sometimes weaves in slightly classical phrases as well. I have a lot of love for his playing. I find myself straying outside the Jerry box from time to time and I'm like "Oh that wasn't quite a Jerry lick, it sounded more like Tony Iommi!" (laughs).

Do you think that the music of Jerry and the Dead has changed at all in terms of how it's being played and interpreted by the bands that do it now?

For sure, look at Dead & Company. It's got a very different feel and it's got a very different tone to it from where they left off in 1995. It's a reinterpretation of that catalog of music, but I don't know that they're looking to make it sound the same. And there are a lot of other bands now. The Skull & Roses Festival in Ventura is a great example. I don't know how many bands they've got on that bill out there, maybe twenty or something, but they all do it a little bit differently. You've got guys like Marcus Rezak who's doing Shred is Dead. He's interpreting Grateful Dead with an edgier kind of vibe to it. Dead music has become a genre. You can take the changes to one of their songs and jam with a group of players and approach it any way you want. I don't tend to listen to too much of that stuff, but it's changed a lot. The musicians I enjoy the most include people like John Kadlecik. He's the coolest. His playing style and vocal style for me is about as close as you're gonna get. It has the real flavor to me of what Garcia was doing. I love Zach Nugent too. He blew me away a couple times this past year. I got to see him at Skull & Roses. He's terrific. He's a young guy. I think he's in his twenties. He doesn't look like a Deadhead but he's in there.

How do you feel about all the bands playing Dead music? Do you ever think it's just too much?

Well, yeah there's a part of me that feels that way. It's a little diluted now. It almost seems like it's more popular now than it's ever been but I also think that it's fantastic too because it keeps the spirit of the music alive. If you've got a room full of people who are there to see that kind of music and the band is able to capture it somehow and connect with the audience, then the magic is there. When this music is done somewhat correctly, it works. There's a little bit of over-saturation yeah, but it's up to the individual bands I think. The individual bands can be really cool or they can be cheap knock-offs. It depends on the group. I would compare GD music to something as large as jazz.

(Garrett Deloian. 2019. Photo by Rich Saputo.)

What do you use in terms of gear when going for the Jerry tone?

There's so much to that world of gear that it took me a lot of years to figure out what I wanted and how to go about it. The guitar that I use primarily these days is a [Gibson] SG that I've modified quite a bit to how Stu Allen modifies his SG. I saw a picture of his wiring somewhere online and it was just super clean the way that he had it all laid out. I wound up sending my guitar to a guy in Cheyenne, Wyoming. His name is Brian White and his company is Io Custom Guitars. He rewired my guitar for me and he also built some real nice brass plates and things like that for its face. Another element to this guitar is the online effects loops that Jerry used. I had one of those installed in the guitar, as well as a buffer made by a guy named Mike Wald. As far as effects I try to just use what Jerry would have used on the particular tunes. I've had a lot of overdrive pedals and what I'm using right now is called a Solar Flare made by Brad Sarno. It's a really dirty distortion overdrive. I've got a Carbon Copy analog delay by MXR. I've got a Boss octave pedal, an MXR Phase and while the Mu-Tron is a vital component to that whole tone right now I'm using the Mu-FX Micro-Tron III, which is a more compact version of the classic Mu-Tron III. I have an actual seventies Mu-Tron III, but it needs some service. For now the micro is getting me through. As far as amps I have tried different things. I know Jerry used a modified Twin but I purchased a FYD amp which is basically just a Twin preamp in a rack mount which I loved though I wasn't crazy about the reverb. A blues artist who is a buddy of mine turned me on to a thing called a Quilter MicroPro Mach 2. I bought one of those and wondered if I could get a Jerry tone out of it. And sure enough the way I have it dialed in I absolutely love it. It's really close. It's great because it's light as can be. You can just throw it in a shoulder bag and take it on an airplane with you. For me, one of the most important pieces of the puzzle is the speaker. These JBL E120s are just the thing man. I've tried a bunch of different speakers, but that's the tone right there. I put two of them in an old Fender speaker cabinet and I mounted skateboard wheels to the side of it to make it easier to transport.

What do you use for guitars?

One of the guitars I have these days is a loaner from a guy named Andy Logan. He's a guitar collector in Redwood City and he owns a ton of beautiful Garcia replicas. He has some Tiger replicas and I think he owns a Rosebud replica. He has a couple of Travis Beans. He owns Jerry's Cripe Saturn guitar. The one that was made by Steven Cripe for Garcia to be next in line after Lightning Bolt and Top Hat. It has two horns on it and it was a guitar that Jerry never played, because Cripe hadn't finished it before he passed away and he never got to deliver it to him. The other guitar I have on loan from him was made by Tom Lieber. Tom Lieber and Doug Irwin built Jerry's Wolf and Tiger guitars together. This one has more of Tiger's shape and style and boy is it a fantastic instrument. And it really does sound like Jerry's. I use it as a backup. I played it full-time for several months, but I've gone back to my SG because I guess that's more my guitar. The playability on the Lieber is much better than the SG, but there's just something tonally with my SG that's a little more personal.

Anything else about Jerry?

I wound up doing this Jerry Garcia thing because of my love for Jerry and the music, but I wouldn't necessarily consider myself a "Grateful Dead guitar player." It's something I can do really proficiently, though I consider myself more of a blues player than a Grateful Dead player, but it all rolls into one.

(Joni Bottari. Photo by James Foster.)

Joni Bottari

Known by some of her fans as "Girl Jerry," Joni Bottari is one of a small number of female artists who pay musical tribute to the playing style of Captain Trips. A native of New Jersey and now a resident of the Sunshine State, Bottari is humble about her well-honed skills on the fretboard and is passionate about producing a convincing Garcia-esque result. As a member of the all-female Grateful Dead tribute band Brown Eyed Women, she brings her talents to a groundbreaking group in a traditionally male-dominated genre.

Hi Joni, are you in Florida?

Yeah, I moved here from New Jersey about twelve years ago.

Is New Jersey where you first started playing?

Yes, as a young girl I really looked up to my brother, Steve. He played in a band on the Jersey Shore during the Springsteen era, in the late sixties and early seventies. They played together on a lot of double bills. I was interested in music and I asked him if I could tag along to some of his rehearsals and he said, "Sure." Then I asked him if he'd teach me how to play guitar. I was about ten at the time. He taught me some first-position chords and how to strum. He was mostly a rhythm player and a songwriter. One day he brought home the albums *Workingman's Dead* and *American Beauty* (1970). It was around the same time I was learning the basics on guitar and I got hooked on the Dead, though I kept calling "Uncle John's Band" Uncle Tom's Cabin. Ha.

Your brother was on bills with the Boss?

Yeah, around '69, '70 and '71. That was when it was just Bruce Springsteen. It wasn't yet Bruce Springsteen and the E-Street Band. I used to see him play at places like my high school auditorium and he would do shows at the Sunshine Inn which was a famous local spot and at the Nothings Festival in 1971. My brother's band and Bruce shared the same sound guy, Tinker [Carl West], who was kind of like the Owsley of New Jersey. They did a lot of festivals together and they rehearsed at Tinker's. So I saw all this going on and I envied and admired my brother. And that's how I got started. My brother had seen the Dead play at the Fillmore East but he wasn't into the scene as much as I was. Once I heard them play, that was it for me.

And you first heard the Dead on vinyl?

Yeah, on what do you call those things again? Oh yeah, turntables. Ha. I think American Beauty came out first and, on its A-side, song one, was "Box of Rain," and I was like, "Wow." At that point they were influenced by the harmonies of Crosby, Stills, Nash and Young and it was acoustic. So that was my intro- duction. I didn't hear stuff like *Live Dead*, with its thirty-minute "Dark Star," until later.

When was your first Dead show?

Well, I wanted to go to Woodstock but my mother wouldn't let me because I was only nine. Later on in 1975, in section two of the *New York Times*, I saw that Jerry was playing with Legion of Mary with Merl Saunders at the Capitol Theatre in Passaic, NJ. I was fourteen at the time. So I stole my mother's Chevy Vega, drove forty miles to see Jerry play with Merl and I went in and sparked up a joint. If I had a fourteen year old like me I'd kill her. I didn't know what I was seeing at the time because there were no bootlegs of Jerry and Merl. The album *Hooteroll* was out but that was about it. But I went, and I was like, "Well these aren't any Dead songs that I know," but I got to see Jerry, so it was great. The Dead were on hiatus that year [1975] except for three shows in California I think, so my first Grateful Dead show wasn't until the lottery shows at the Beacon Theatre in 1976. You couldn't get a ticket so I paid an usher off to let me in. I was fifteen and I'd stolen my mother's car (again) and driven to Manhattan. I went with Dave Margulies, who now runs High Sierra Music. He didn't get in. But yeah I paid the usher off with ten bucks and I walked in and that was my first Dead show. I was shocked that it worked.

When you first started playing your guitar early on did you know how to play any Dead tunes?

I did but I was in a band at the time with Steve and John Conte. They've played with a lot of people. John Conte is the bass player with Southside Johnny and the Asbury Jukes now. We had a little band, but if you're playing with non-Deadheads and you don't sing, you don't really have the power to call the songs. We played a lot of Chuck Berry and Rolling Stones and Beatles and stuff like that. It was around 1973 or 1974. We played at our high schools and friends' bar mitzvahs. Then I went to college and after college in 1982 I moved back to New York City, where I answered an ad in the *Village Voice* for an all-fe- male band that played at CBGB and clubs like that. They were looking for a lead guitar player and I got the gig. I played in that band for three years, performing all around the East Village doing all-original music. Again, I would have loved to play Dead but that's just not where I landed. Then I got severe stage fright around 1985 when the band was splitting up. I was throwing up and I was terrified. When that band broke up I said, "That's it I'll never play in public again." And I didn't for twenty-two years. I always had stage fright but it got to the point where it paralyzed me and even a Valium or a drink wouldn't take the fear out of me so I just said, "I can't do this." I could play at home and for friends and my dog, but I couldn't play in public.

But you started playing again as part of a Grateful Dead cover band in Florida?

Yeah, I moved down here because my mom was sick and there was a Grateful Dead band called Crazy Fingers that's been playing for a long time in South Florida. I used to go see them when I'd come down and visit but they didn't really know me. One night I went to one of their shows and I thought to myself that I'd like to sit in and play a song one day if I could. So I contacted a guy who used to be in the band. He'd shown up for their twentieth anniversary gig thing that I'd seen on YouTube and he was a rhythm player. I just wanted to jam with this guy in his man cave. So I called him and said, "Hey my name's Joni, I play a little Jerry and I just want to jam." Here I am thinking, "Oh god this guy is going to think I'm coming on to him." And he was like "Ok." And one of the other guys from Crazy Fingers, who has since passed away, was there too when I went over and I think they thought it was going to be a joke. Like, "Haha there's a girl coming over. A girrrl! And she said blah blah blah!" So I go over with my little Vox amp that had an auto-wah on it, just a little tiny amp and I started playing "Shakedown" and they just looked at each other. And believe me I don't have any ego. I'm not fooling myself. Half the time I want to throw my guitar out the fucking window you know. I want to hear Mattson or someone play. And they're like, "Oh shit, she can play!" So the rhythm guy said, "We gotta start a band!" And I was like "No. You don't understand I don't play in public." And he was like, "Are you kidding?! You're the only girl Jerry in the country! You have to! There's nobody else." And he goes, "I can verify this through GratefulDeadTributeBands.com." So I was like, "That's great but I'm not doing it." After a month of trying to convince me to do it I finally agreed. They even had a stand-by for me in case I bailed. The first show was May 4, 2012, at the Funky Biscuit in Boca Raton. I was a nervous wreck for a week before the gig. We played it as part of the band Unlimited Devotion, which is a group I started with that guy. So I did it for like a year-and-a-half and it was a little rough around the edges because though I'd played all the music in my head, it's different when you're out there. Eventually I quit and started playing with some singer-songwriters and then I put the acoustic Girl Jerry band together, which was good but I couldn't do stuff like a "Playin' in the Band" jam and get lost in it or a "ChinaRider" and really take it out there, so I ended that and started Spiral Light, which I've had for the past year-and-a-half with some players who all know the music. And now the Brown Eyed Women thing is just a dream come true.

Spiral Light was your band? And Girl Jerry too?

Yeah, Girl Jerry was a project I tried. It was good. We did some Old & In the Way. We did some acoustic and some electric but not everyone was a Deadhead so I could only go so far with it and get off so much. So that's why I started Spiral Light and then the whole Brown Eyed Women thing just exploded last month.

How'd you connect with the other members of Brown Eyed Women?

Well every now and then people would call me up and say, "Hey you were mentioned on Sirius Radio," because I'd played a house party with David Gans and he knew of me. And people would call

SiriusXM and say, "How come there aren't any female Jerry players?" and David would say, "There is one, her name's Joni." That happened like five times. Then my phone would blow up and I'd go, "That's cool." But the last time he got one of those calls he mentioned another girl's name Denise Parent. So I go on Facebook and discover she's the drummer of the Deadbeats in Woodstock. So I message her on Facebook and I go, "Hey we both got a shout-out today," and then we chatted on the phone. I check out her playing and I see she's really solid on drums and she sings. I always had a dream to be in an all-female Dead band, but I couldn't even find a keyboardist who sings within a hundred-mile radius. I'd made friends with a bass player from Jersey online, Dana, from Lovelight, and I played with a girl from Boston who plays keyboards and who flew down once and there's a phenomenal singer in Pittsburgh in a band called theCAUSE. But I was kinda like, "Oh well, it's probably not going to happen." About a month later Denise calls me back and says, "I talked to everyone and they're interested." Then I got a call from a girl from Atlanta who plays like Bobby. So we started having these conference calls every week and I'm thinking that we live in six different states, we've never played together, we don't have any video…how are we gonna get a gig?! I called a friend down here who knows some venue owners and he called some club owners and they loved the concept, everyone loved the concept, and that's how we were able to put a five-show tour (June 26-June 30, 2019) in Florida together. That's how it got off the ground. Everyone flew in from the Northeast. It was a lot of logistics. It was a lot of work, but it was pretty epic with big turnouts and then last week SiriusXM played our version of "Brown Eyed Women" on the air during the Tales from the Golden Road radio show. And we've been interviewed a couple times on the show now.

Hey, if people know their Dead music it can work without too much rehearsing…

Yeah, we had Google Docs going too. Like, "What version of 'Let it Grow' are we gonna do? The '77 version? Do you want to do this change in 'China>Rider?' Do you want to go to double time? Should we play 'Ship of Fools' in the album key or the live key?" That kind of stuff needs to be worked out. We had a conference call like almost every week.

It's a language, if people speak it, more or less you can wing it…

Exactly, that's why I've disbanded other projects, because not everyone spoke the same language.

How do people react to the all-female presentation of Grateful Dead music?

So far we've had nothing but amazing feedback. Is it a novelty? Is it a shtick? Of course it is to a certain degree, but it would be different if none of us could play. Everyone in the group is in a band in their own town and has been doing this for years. Denise has played more than four thousand shows and has been playing for more than twenty-five years. Everyone is a pro. I heard one guy say, "Well when you said Girl Jerry I was thinking whatever, but I came and heard you and was like damn she can play!" All these women can play!

Are you a strict interpreter of Jerry?

My approach to playing is . . . Jerry rips man. If I could play like a Jeff Mattson, for example, I would, but it's hard. I put my own spin on it with some blues and some bends and stuff like that, because I can do myself better than I can do me trying to be exactly like Jerry. I think some people cop out and say, "Oh I'm not Bob Weir and I don't try to be." Well you know why? Because they don't put a lot of time into it. It's much easier to be themselves because if you want to play how Rob Eaton covers

(Joni with her Wolf guitar. Photo courtesy of Joni Bottari.)

Bob, or Tom Circosta [of the Zen Tricksters], it takes a lifetime of work. It's hard as hell to learn all those Bobby voicings. So my honest answer is I'll do a signature lick and then I do my own thing.

The Dead don't get as much credit as they should for being amazingly good musicians . . .

Yeah, I try and study it so that I can hit the signature parts in every song and I want to come as close to Jerry as is within my abilities. I would rather see a band that can sound like the Dead versus just inter-pretation, with some exceptions. I think JRAD does a great job and they totally go off and do their own thing. They're like the Dead on steroids and Joe Russo reminds me of Keith Moon. He's just a wild man, he's great. But call me crazy, when I see a tribute band I want to see someone who sounds like the actual band. I try not to say too much on Facebook anymore, because it's almost like politics on some of these groups. People will be like, "Why do you have to sound like Jerry? Just be yourself. Jerry sounded like himself." And sometimes I just want to say, "Motherfucker because you can't." I can't always pull off a lot of shred like on "Morning Dew," which is really slow song. The slower the song the harder it can be. When I know I can't pull it off I just go into Joni mode and do what I can. I have soft hands and I try to play pretty. I try to listen to what everyone else is playing and not just be on my own island.

I see that you have a Jerry-style guitar . . .

Yeah I have a Jerry Wolf guitar but the mother-of-pearl inlay on mine actually looks like a [German] Shepherd, and that was for my old dog, Jerry. It was made by Pat O'Donnell of Resurrection Guitars who took over for Steve Cripe when he died. Pat lived in the same town that Cripe lived in [in Florida]. When Cripe died the guys who built my guitar went in, with permission, and took the wood that was also used for Jerry's TopHat. I think it was East Indian rosewood that had been part of an opium bed. He made around six Tiger-style guitars out of that block of wood and those guitars go up in price every year. But I figured I don't need a Tiger and I don't need that wood, because I knew it would raise the price a lot, but I wanted a Wolf and and I wanted my dog as the inlay. A lot of the guitars he makes have the wolf as the battery cover, which is raised, but I wanted my battery in the back and I wanted a flush wolf that looked like my dog on the front. I have the same schematics and the same pickups as the other Wolf guitars, the only thing that's different is I don't have a volume knob for the middle pickup. I was very specific about the weight, using cherry wood instead of purpleheart to make it lighter, because I don't want to carry around a nine- or ten-pound guitar. I'm really pleased with it.

Did you study music formally?

No. Though when my mother passed away in 2006 I didn't know what to do with myself so I watched a lot of YouTube instructional videos. I watched Seth Fleishman. He's the man. You have to pay for his lessons. I started getting into that. Then when I started playing again I started getting into gear.

What gear did you get into?

Well, I didn't go crazy and get the JBL speakers and the Hard Trucker cabinets, but I got my Jerry guitar and an original Mu-Tron III envelope filter calibrated by Richard Lingenberg. I mean, how could you play "Shakedown Street," or "Ramble On Rose," or "Catfish John," without it?! I also have an octave divider, which you need for songs like "Feel Like a Stranger," and I put my pedalboard together with a pedal power supply by Voodoo Lab and the overdrive from Sarno and the phaser for "Candyman," and "West L.A. Fadeaway," and two delays, with one on all the time and one for when you want a lot of repeats.

So you're going for the Jerry tone . . .

Tone is important, though I don't take it to the degree of some people. You know Jerry's McIntosh was three hundred watts. You can't push three hundred watts in a small venue to make it break up. You could do it at Giants Stadium, but you can't do that at the local bar. Jerry had that clean tone and when it would break up at a certain point, it would sound great which is what you want. But he had to push that amp, and you just can't do that at small places.

What are you using for an amp?

I'm a really big fan right now of the Quilters. So I switch between a Quilter with an extension cab and a Fender concert amp with four tens, which are the original Fender speakers. It's a brownface. It's heavy and I'm in my fifties so what I use depends on the show. I have the Quilter MicroPro MP200-8. Quilter makes both combo amps and heads.

How do you feel about the fact that there are so many Dead-inspired bands these days?

I think it's cool. The only thing that isn't great is when there are so many of them that the venues play the bands against each other. It hurts some acts because other bands will take a gig for less money and the owners can take advantage of that in certain markets. It can be territorial, awkward and not totally Dead-like all the time. It becomes a business. But it's a phenomenon like the world has never seen. I mean there was the Beatles and Elvis, but neither of those artists played for thirty years. You had Elvis impersonators but you didn't have Elvis heads going from show to show. So there's nothing to compare it to. You have kids now who weren't born when Jerry was alive and they know the words to every song.

Andrea Whitt. Photo by Rich Saputo.

Andrea Whitt

The impressively talented Andrea Whitt is known to some Deadheads through her playing with the Acid Americana duo Katie & Andrea. Whitt's Garcia-inspired pedal steel guitar work is matched only by her skills as a fashion blogger, illustrator and multi-instrumentalist. She has traveled with Dead & Company and provided her fiddle and viola chops for artists including Shania Twain and Kendrick Lamar. Her strength lies in soulful musicianship, creativity and an upbeat approach to whatever life brings.

Can you tell me a little about your background?

I grew up in Columbus, Ohio, where I started playing music on viola (a stringed instrument in the violin family) when I was nine. I got into fiddle playing about six years ago when I joined Shania Twain's band. I played in her band on fiddle and viola and we had a pedal steel player in that group. I was so intrigued by the pedal steel that I ordered one off of eBay and had it sent to my hotel room in Las Vegas. The first thing that I wanted to learn was Jerry's solo over "Dire Wolf." So I kind of taught myself pedal steel from transcribing all of Jerry's intros and solos from the Grateful Dead staples that have pedal steel in them. I'd watch videos and take "Dire Wolf" and slow it down by twenty-five percent and through trial and error I'd figure out which pedal and which string did what. I taught myself pedal steel by studying Jerry Garcia.

Was your family musical?

No one really played music as a full-time career, but my grandfather played piano for the silent movie theaters. He also owned newspapers and was a journalist. Music was just one of many things he did, but he was a great composer and improviser. My aunt was an incredible self-taught guitar player but she went into nursing. My family is incredibly supportive of what I do. My mom is a huge music fan and she introduced me to a lot of styles of music growing up.

How'd you first come to hear Jerry's music?

I was around twelve or thirteen and my cousin, who I looked up to for stuff like what kind of new and hip music to check out, liked the Dead and the Doors and a lot of classic rock. I started listening through her. I bought a bunch of CDs from BMG Music Service where you could buy like ten CDs for a penny. A couple of the discs I ordered were *Workingman's Dead* and *Skeleton's From the Closet*. I listened to those on repeat for years. I would play them non-stop and those were the only songs I knew from the Dead for a while. There's so much pedal steel on *Workingman's Dead* and I just had to learn those songs because that was what I loved growing up. About twelve years ago I played in a group that was kind of a jammy band and we played a few Dead songs, but I took on Jerry's playing when I got into steel guitar about six years ago.

(Andrea on pedal steel. Photo by Rich Saputo.)

Have you tried playing the Jerry pedal steel parts on "Teach Your Children?"

Yeah, Katie [Skene] and I are actually going to try and film our version of that for Jerry Week [2019]. I've learned all those licks.

Do you think of yourself as a Deadhead?

I was thirteen when Jerry passed away so I never made it to a Grateful Dead show, but yeah definitely. Katie and I [toured and performed in the VIP areas as part of Loose Lucy's Lounge] with Dead & Company [in 2019] and before that I went to three days of Dead50 in Chicago. I had also taken in a few scattered Dead & Company shows before Katie and I jumped on the recent tour. But yeah, on this last tour we stood side-stage and watched all the shows. It's pretty cool coming from being a fan when you're twelve to where you're actually standing on the side of the stage for every show.

How'd you get in with Dead & Company?

Well, Katie and [former Grateful Dead roadie] Steve Parish were doing a handful of shows earlier this year where Steve would tell Grateful Dead stories [on The Big Steve Hour] and Katie would play songs to go along with it. Steve might tell the tale behind how the song "Cassidy" came about and then Katie would play a version of the song. They did that for a while and they did a mini tour. And then Katie and I put together a bunch of songs for the Skull & Roses Festival [in 2019]. From that Steve asked us to go on tour with Dead & Company to play the VIP lounges. That's kind of how that all rolled. They tried to figure out how to fit us in and the VIP lounges turned out to be the place.

How does that work?

People pay a lot of money for a VIP ticket, mostly for early access to the pit. But there was never any live entertainment, just snacks and stuff. There was no meet-and-greet. Maybe they got like a poster or a spot on the rail. So this added a fun musical element to the experience.

How did it go?

We were well received. Everyone was so warm and it was great to see their reactions. As a duo it's tricky to pull together songs and hold it together, but people loved it. I was very happy to be part of it.

Did you have a big repertoire?

I think we came in with thirty songs on our list. And on any given night we'd play about six songs. So, we'd have the ones that were really tight and we'd get a great response from that. And we'd try new stuff. "Dire Wolf" is always a favorite. "Candyman" is fun. "Sugar Magnolia" was on the list. "To Lay Me Down." "High Time." " 'Til the Morning Comes." "Ramble on Rose." We tried to do some stuff that people don't always play.

Did you do any space jams?

We played in between when Steve would speak, so we didn't have a ton of room to get too weird. It was more like a casual thing, so we kept it to songs. The tour was seventeen-shows long and we did eight of those seventeen shows. We did the California shows and then some shows in New York, Camden, Boston and Wrigley Field.

Are you familiar with some of the newer Dead-related cover bands?

We're friends with Jerry's Middle Finger, and I'm going to see JRAD for the first time when they come to L.A. in a few weeks. I met [JRAD guitarist] Tom Hamilton at Dead & Company.

What other kind of music do you like?

I studied jazz in college and I listened to a lot of jazz. I also played a lot of Brazilian jazz and I've listened to a lot of Charlie Parker and a bunch of saxophone players. To be honest, I've also listened to a lot of the Dave Matthews Band and I still like that. I know a lot of people think that Dave Matthews is meaningless pop, but they sound fantastic right now.

Can you talk a little bit about what you use in terms of gear?

I use a Strymon El Capistan dTape Echo Pedal for delay. I like the tape echo a lot. And I use a Bubble Tron Dynamic Flanger Phaser pedal made by Robert Keeley. I use it on tunes like "Candyman." It can do phase, flange and filter – I can tweak between the three. It makes everything very bubbly. I like putting it on the phase setting. I also have a Wampler Tumnus overdrive. It's a mini pedal that I use for overdrive. I love it. I have a vintage fuzz pedal that I don't even know who made it. It's all faded. I like putting fuzz in there. I also have an EP Booster pedal by Xotic. That pedal saved my ass this summer. I put it before my volume pedal and it boosts the signal and gives it a clean and sparkly lift. For the shows we played, the sound was not that thought out, so it helped. I use a Rivera tube amp. I also run through an L.R. Baggs preamp. Although pedal steel fits in both electric and acoustic formats, it always needs to be amplified.

Do you do anything special to try and achieve Jerry's sound when you play pedal steel?

He had a very specific way of blocking notes with his right hand. It's more about attack. Like how hard he's picking the notes and when he's blocking them and how much he lets the notes ring. That's more the Jerry approach than anything else. It's the right-hand technique more than anything. He was missing his middle finger. Normally the third pick goes on your middle finger so he had to move it down to his ring finger.

How do you feel about all the bands that cover this music? It seems like Dead-related music is getting played as much as ever now . . .

I'm glad it's moving people enough for them to go out and perform it. It means a lot to me, so I'm happy that other people are getting the same use from it. To be able to internalize it and then put it back out into the world is wonderful. I think it's great. The more the merrier. I suppose if it really sucks, well . . . (laughs). Honestly, as long as people's hearts are in the right place it's all good.

(Vic DeRobertis. Somerville. 2020. Photo by Matt Beauchemin)

Vic DeRobertis

Vic DeRobertis first appeared on this author's Dead radar sometime in 1995, when he was a member of Uncle John's Band in the Tampa Bay area. Nowadays Vic performs in New England as part of the group Playing Dead. Watching him play, one is immediately struck by his attention to detail and his easy delivery. Having studied the sound and sense of Garcia, DeRobertis creates Grateful Dead-inspired music in a way that makes audiences remember why they fell in love with the band in the first place. He took in his first Dead shows in the late seventies and proceeded to absorb the music into his very being. DeRobertis does this all while bringing the experience into full psychedelic life as a left-handed guitarist.

Where did you grow up and when did you start playing?

I grew up in Scarsdale, New York, in Westchester County, which is just north of New York City. I was always musical. We had a piano in the house and I'd bang away on it as a little kid. I think I took about two months worth of lessons. The teacher wanted me to learn "Flight of the Bumblebee" and I wanted to learn how to play "Benny and the Jets," so that didn't really work out. I more or less taught myself on piano, and a little later, in sixth grade, I took up the drums. I was a drummer throughout high school. I didn't start playing the guitar until I was around the age of sixteen, when I found one in the attic of our house that had belonged to my older sister. I figured out how to play a G chord on it immediately. That was the impetus of the whole thing. But I picked it up backwards. I picked it up left-handed. I played it up upside down and learned my first chord. It was a terrible guitar, with nylon strings and a really wide nut, that was hard to use.

Are you a natural lefty?

I'm ambidextrous, but I felt more comfortable playing lefty. Funny thing is that when I was in eighth grade I got a poster of Jerry. This would have been back in 1977 or so, but he was playing his Wolf guitar and the image had been flipped so it looked like he was playing left-handed. I didn't notice that for years. But if you think about playing piano, which is where I started, your right hand is doing the more intricate stuff and your left hand is kind of playing bass notes. So if you flip the piano around like a guitar, since I play lefty, my right hand is doing all the fretting which feels very natural.

43

Did your parents or anyone else in your family play music?

Nobody. We had the piano in the living room because that's what you have, but it was that thing in the corner that nobody ever played. I guess my sister had tried to play the guitar at one point, but she gave it up.

How'd you first come to hear the music of Jerry and the Dead?

When I was about eleven or twelve I was into the music that all the other kids were listening to at the time, like Led Zeppelin, Aerosmith, Bad Company and a little bit of Yes. But one day I was going through my older sister's record collection down in the basement and I found a copy of *Europe '72*. I put it on and it was during "Jack Straw" that my dials lit up. My sister had never really been a big Deadhead, but some of my friends had older siblings who turned them onto the Dead, although this was before they were very popular. At that point the band was doing some live FM broadcasts of their shows from the Capitol Theatre in Passaic, NJ. The local radio station WNEW would simulcast the shows and we got some exposure that way. Also my friends and I would hang out at this high-end stereo store, probably annoying the hell out of the guy who owned it, but he had a reel-to-reel on which he had recorded the Felt Forum show from Dec. 10, 1971, when it was broadcast live, and it was a great recording of it. We'd go there and force him to put it on. We absorbed it anyway we could. This was before I started playing guitar, but I started to get a pretty good tape collection going and I saw my first show in 1978, when I was about fifteen.

Where was the show?

It was at Giants Stadium at the Meadowlands. It was a show that they used to help fund their trip to Egypt.

Who were some of your other musical influences from that time?

I was into all the popular bands of the day. I was really into Jimmy Page as I said. I still am, I love his guitar playing. But I was also into the Allman Brothers, Marshall Tucker, Lynyrd Skynyrd and all those bands that were coming up.

Has your musical taste changed much since then?

Good question. I don't really listen to much classic rock anymore and I very rarely really listen to the Grateful Dead these days. I got such a solid jolt of it from around the age of sixteen to about when I was twenty-two. I listened to almost nothing else during that time, and I saw a whole lot of Grateful Dead shows between 1978 and 1985. I probably saw the Dead around eighty times plus a lot of Jerry Garcia Band shows. I had a big tape collection and I had good connections for first-generation soundboards and all that kind of stuff. So it's all in my head now. I can pretty much dial up any tape I want to in my mind. Which I think has a lot to do with the way that I approach this music. I don't find that I need to practice anything or work on it much. It's sort of all in there, in my brain. It annoys the hell out of my bandmates. They'll be messing with their iPads and trying to remember stuff that I can just recall. I don't have trouble remembering lyrics or chord changes even if we haven't played a song in years.

So you have a photographic memory of sorts?

For lyrics and chords changes I seem to. I can even remember words to theme songs from the seventies with no trouble, which is a pretty useless talent.

What about Jerry and the Dead do you like? What pulled you in?

You know I wouldn't have necessarily called myself a Deadhead until I went to that first show at the Meadowlands in '78 when I caught some nice versions of "Fire on the Mountain" and "Good Lovin' " that just seeped into my brain. I started singing them when I was walking home from school and stuff like that. They got in there real deep. Two days after that [Dead] show I went and saw Yes and I was thoroughly unimpressed. It just wasn't the same vibe or the same feeling. Later on I caught some of the Dead's legendary Radio City Music Hall shows [in 1980]. It was such a friendly scene. It felt very intimate. You felt like you were among one big family and it was really appealing. When the band got more popular their shows started getting bigger, crazier and seedier, but I always loved that feeling that I got as a young Deadhead back in the day. I used to drive all over the place to see them. I was still catching smaller shows even in the later eighties, but it got harder to get tickets. After 1985 I didn't go as regularly. I did take in a nice pair of shows in 1988 at the Bay Front Center in St. Petersburg, Fla., which was about a four-thousand seat venue I think. There were a lot of people looking for tickets

(Vic DeRobertis channeling Jerry left-handed. Marlboro. 2019.
Photo by Matt Beauchemin.)

and I happened to have an extra. I was having a really good time. I had just taken a really difficult general knowledge editing test for a job that I was applying for at a newspaper in Memphis, and one of the questions on the test was to name as many of the seven dwarves as you could. So when I was outside the venue

45

in St. Pete I offered to sell my extra ticket at face value if someone could name all seven dwarves. It was really entertaining. Nobody could do it. Most people couldn't recall much past Sleepy and Grumpy. And everybody totally forgot about Doc. Finally I just gave the ticket to a pretty girl. Another fun memory from those shows is that I couldn't decide whether I wanted to take that job in Memphis or not, so I decided that if they played any songs about Tennessee I'd take the job. They played "Tennessee Jed" and "Stuck Inside of Mobile," so I wound up taking the gig.

Are you trained in music theory at all?

No. I know jack shit about theory. It's probably my biggest weakness, or maybe it's good for me. Who knows? but I don't think about scales, I don't think about modes. I just play by ear. I know I'm playing the correct scales and I know I'm playing the correct modes, but I don't have any frame of reference to know what any of that stuff is. I don't really look at the fretboard very much when I play. It's like my hand just knows what to do.

Amazing, I would have figured you were dialed in on all that because your style seems so precise . . .

Yeah, it's just intuitive to me. It's weird I know, but I can't tell you what scale I'm playing. I don't think it has hurt me one bit. People argue about is that Mixolydian or is that Dorian. It's all Greek to me no pun intended, I just play what sounds right to my ear.

Did you consider yourself a Deadhead?

Yeah by my second or third show I was on the bus for sure. It was all I wanted to do and all I would listen to. I was driving long distances with five friends crammed into a tiny car for twelve hours to see a show. I never went on tour per se, but when they came to the East Coast I'd see maybe six, seven or eight shows in a row, though I never gave up everything and went to sell grilled cheese sandwiches in the parking lot. I mainly wanted to listen to the music and get up close so I could hear it well and see what was going on. For the large percentage of the shows I took in I was pretty straight. I did my share of partying here and there but I was never that into getting really high or really fucked up or taking too much of anything. A little bit was always good just to open my ears a bit. At one show in 1980 at Rochester, some guy handed me a piece of paper and then was like, "Oh wait don't take that one." It was right out of Cheech and Chong. Too late, I had taken it. That was about as high as I ever got. I remember they played "Aiko Aiko" and "Morning Dew." It was a great show and I actually managed to record it. But for the most part I was fine with just a little bit of a buzz and enjoying the music.

Do you think the music has changed at all since Jerry passed, with all these new bands taking on the repertoire?

It's been interesting to see the various interpretations of it since 1995. Starting with the direction Phil took it using different players with more organized jams and using directed key changes and stuff. And then of course what Bobby did with it in RatDog, though some of the tempos got excruciatingly slow there. But yeah it's totally cool what the different guitarists have brought to it. I saw a few great Phil Lesh & Friends shows in 2000, with Warren Haynes and Jimmy Herring, Rob Barraco on keys and John Molo on drums. It was amazing to see how they approached it. I loved Warren's singing. Nobody sings a Jerry ballad like he does. And the guitar playing was interesting and outside of the usual Grateful Dead realm. It was really tasty with bluesy riffs that had more of an Allman Brothers feel to it. So yeah the different interpretations have been cool. I think John Mayer does a nice job as well. He has studied Garcia obviously and he has a really good understanding of what Jerry is up to and he's referencing some of the signature parts, which often are missing when other people are doing these tunes. To me that's very important.

(Vic and Playing Dead at the Regent Theater in Arlington, MA. Photo by Matt Beauchemin.)

Do you think there are too many Dead-inspired acts out there now?

Good question, there are probably like thirty of them in Boston now. I've been playing lead for my band, Playing Dead, since about 2003. There might have been one other Dead band around when we started. Now it has just exploded. There's a different Grateful Dead cover band playing every weekend here. Some of them are really good and some of them are not so good. And some of them are taking the music and completely reinterpreting it. There's even a band here that plays a hard rock version of "China Doll."

What do you look for when you're watching a Dead cover band?

When I'm listening to a Dead cover band I'm listening for the interplay between the rhythm guitar, the bass, the keyboards and the lead guitar and I'm listening for those signature parts to fit together to make the song. In some bands you can hear it happening and in other bands it's not there at all. It's almost like they're oblivious to it. I'm not sure if many of the people who go to see these bands really know the difference. They just want to hear some band rockin' out on "Bertha." They don't give a shit if the band is doing the rolling accents during the solos. They don't care if the lead guitar player is playing the solo that Jerry played the same every time. They're not cognizant of it. That's the stuff that lights my dials up though … you hear those little sonic references when guys like John Kadlecik and Jeff Mattson are playing. You kind of absorb it through your DNA from listening at an early age and it just comes out. But it doesn't seem to bother anybody if it isn't there. And it doesn't mean that those bands aren't having a good time or that people aren't enjoying it. I mean at what level do you judge it? Nobody is as good as Jerry. Period. I can give you dozens of spots I look for watching a Dead cover band. Does the lead guitar player reach down to flick the envelope filter on and off during the verses of "Estimated Prophet" the way Jerry did? Is he palming the pick so he can fingerpick the intro to "Althea" and then switching back to the pick for the leads? Does he turn the octave divider on instead of the envelope filter for the second verse of "Feel Like a Stranger?" These are all tiny nuances that Jerry would do – every time.

What gear do you favor when going for the Jerry tone?

About ten years ago, I went through an equipment change. I was hauling around a hundred-pound 2x12 Hard Truckers cabinet with the E120s and I had a pedal drawer and a preamp and the reverb and the power amp and everything, and I threw it all away and now I just use a Fractal Audio AX8 [amp modeler and effects processor]. I modeled my E120 cabinet by recording it and making IRs [sound patches], which have spread pretty far around the internet. I think a lot of people use my cabinet patch now. I did the effects one at a time and I did the preamp and I did the reverb and that's all I use. It goes direct to the front of the house and I have a powered monitor full range in front of me that I'm hearing, and that's it.

So you don't need all that stuff anymore?

I don't need nothin' anymore. I just walk in with my guitar in my one hand and this little eight-pound floor board in the other and plug it in and the tone is the same every night and at every venue. And that was the whole point of doing it. I had been carrying around great big heavy cabinets with a lot of power and a lot of cables and a lot of effects. I mean it's too fucking loud for most venues and you're killing people and killing yourself. And depending on the venue you were usually fighting it. I remember playing this bar near Boston where they had this brick wall right behind the stage and my cabinet would be sitting two feet away from that brick wall and my sound would be ungodly bright, so I'd have to turn the bright switch off or turn the treble way down so it would sound good onstage, but that was messing with what was going to the front of the house. So now I've got it all modeled to my ear and to my liking and I know that when I hand an XLR cable to the sound guy that the exact tone that I want is going to be the tone that's coming out of the PA. The "serious" guys would call me a heretic for not using the exact gear Jerry hauled around and – gasp! – going digital – but, hey, Garcia had Steve Parish to carry everything.

What are you playing guitar-wise now?

I play kind of a bare-bones copy of Jerry's Tiger guitar, which is to say it has a cocobolo top, maple back and a maple neck. I didn't do a lot of the ornamentation on it. So, I didn't do the inlay or the cocobolo on the back of the guitar. I didn't do the brass. It has the shape and the tone and the woods that I was after. That's my primary guitar. It's pretty heavy at ten pounds. It's a one-trick pony. It sounds like Jerry's guitar and that's pretty much all it does. I have a Scott Walker guitar that is my backup that also works real well. But I rarely play it. Mostly I play the Tiger. If a battery goes out I'll pick up the Walker.

(Katie Skene. Photo by Rich Saputo.)

Katie Skene

G rowing up in North Florida, Katie Skene took some of her early musical cues from her older brother who was a disciple of Southern rock and the blues, and her mother who listened to classic folk-inspired artists. Skene moved out to the West Coast eventually and found herself in the jamband scene, falling in with groups such as California Kind, which includes guitar virtuoso Barry Sless and talented keyboardist Rob Barraco. The 26-year-old songwriter and guitar player released the first EP of her own material in 2016 right after graduating from USC. Today she tours with the duo Katie & Andrea and plays her own music when not performing moving covers of Grateful Dead songs.

You were one of the first musicians who came to mind when I thought of female artists who have been influenced by Jerry and the Dead. There aren't really that many women on the Dead jamming scene . . .

Yeah, Andrea [Whitt] and I have talked about that. We definitely realized it when we played at the Skull & Roses Festival recently. There weren't really any other female artists playing instruments. There were a few women singing here and there. It was an interesting realization.

Are you from Florida originally?

Yeah, I grew up in Tallahassee. My parents moved to Florida from Virginia when I was about five or six.

Did you start playing down there?

Yes, my big brother, who is six years older, picked up the guitar and started getting into playing through some friends. First he was into the normal rock stuff, and then the blues scene became a part of our lives. A good friend of his, Luke Walton, who is about to start touring with Jimmy Herring's new band, The 5 of 7, was very close to my brother and he introduced him to music by the Allman Brothers, Stevie Ray Vaughan, Albert King and that kind of stuff. From there, I decided that I wanted to pick up the guitar and so those were some of the first artists that I was exposed to in guitar world. There's a really great blues scene down in Tallahassee. Because my brother was playing on that scene, when I got to be old enough, around fourteen or fifteen, I got to sit in with some of the local players at the open jams or they would let me sit in wherever they were playing. So that's how I started. By the time I was sixteen or seventeen I was jamming all the time.

Were you singing too?

Yeah, I learned the ropes playing a lot of rhythm guitar and some of the older guys asked me to sing in their bands too. So I played a lot of rhythm and sang backups as well as singing lead on some songs. We did all sorts of stuff by the Rolling Stones, Muddy Waters, Johnny Winter and the Allman Brothers. The normal stuff you would hear down there. That's how I cut my teeth.

How'd you first come to hear the music of the Grateful Dead?

My parents weren't really Deadheads but I got really into music when I was in high school and they were really into the folk music of the sixties and seventies, which I loved. Stuff like Joni Mitchell. She's my favorite songwriter. But the only Grateful Dead record that my mom had was *Workingman's Dead* and she just loved it. She loved "Uncle John's Band. " That was her favorite song and she'd be like, "You gotta hear this song!" So that was one of the first songs by the Dead that I heard. I got more and more into it from there. And this might be sacrilege, but I was always more influenced by the albums. I really dug the songs. I thought I was deep into at the time but I was really just in the shallow waters. When I came out to school in California to study music at USC I got really into songwriting and when I started analyzing these Dead songs I realized how amazing each composition was. Nothing about them is typical, so I fell more and more in love with it. It was gradual over the years. And when I fell in with John Molo and Barry Sless, Pete Sears and Rob Barraco, they brought me up to Terrapin Crossroads and all of a sudden I was on the fast-track to learning about all the different eras of the Grateful Dead. It was a revelation. It's been an education with them over the past few years. I thought I was a Deadhead and I thought I knew the songs in the catalog, but I discovered that I had a lot more to learn. And I've been learning ever since.

So initially you were into classic blues?

Yeah, definitely. I liked B.B. King a lot and the Delta Blues too. Bessie Smith changed my world when I heard her sing. I also like electric Chicago blues a lot. Artists like Howlin' Wolf and Hubert Sumlin were some of the first soloists I learned from. I also love Eric Clapton and Duane Allman. *Layla* is my favorite album. I love the combination of songwriting and guitar playing and how quickly that all happened on a whim over a few days in Miami at Criteria Studios – with Clapton running into Duane Allman and asking him to come in and play on his album and the birth of that record and just how much amazing content came out of it. That's the beauty of music. Just going with things and being inspired in the moment. Which is very much a Grateful Dead thing too.

Has your musical taste changed at all as you've gotten older?

It has. I don't go back and listen to all the things that first inspired me so much now. Though I did have a little bit of fun playing some stuff I learned from Hubert Sumlin and Howlin' Wolf just the other night. My taste has come a long way, but all that stuff sticks in your head so much that you don't have to listen to it every day to remember it. When I moved to California I hadn't really checked out Neil Young that much though I was a big Joni Mitchell fan as I mentioned earlier. When I moved out here there was all this music that I started getting into. I became more interested and more dedicated to songwriting. It really changed the way I listen to music in general. My taste is basically the same, but the umbrella of Americana takes in a lot. The world has sort of shrunk. You can catch a very diverse group of artists at any one festival these days. I think that people's tastes have broadened. If it's really good music then people who appreciate good music will like it.

Was there anything about Jerry's music that stood out to you?

Well the songs were so haunting. What he did with Robert Hunter is unbelievable. I mean something like "Brokedown Palace" is one of my favorite compositions ever. When you go to learn it it's just amazing. It starts in one key and ends in another. The melodies are incredible. I don't co-write very much, but the trust that they had in each other is just mind-blowing to me. Also Jerry's melodic content on the guitar playing is incredible. If you want to get really nerdy, I love his bends. They're not like anyone else. The only person I can think of who has a bend in that same realm is Albert King. And what he does, because his guitar is upside down, is he bends down from the top. Jerry doesn't do that but he gets the same stanky, twangy sound. I don't know how he does it. I'm learning a lot of his melodic lines. I don't have Jerry's vocabulary the way that some of the guys who have been emulating him for years do. Some of those licks aren't in my arsenal, but I'm learning a lot of them. But something like those bends are one thing, from my blues playing, that I can try and throw in right away.

Are you playing a lot of lead guitar these days?

I've always played some lead, though in some of the bands I play with, such as California Kind, I don't need to play a lot of lead because Barry Sless has a prominent lead role there and then someone like Rob Barraco on keys is right there following that. They're like a school of fish the way they can respond to each other. But they'll let me step out on certain songs that I want to try. They're gracious about it. I love playing rhythm too. It influences what other people are going to play on top of it. I get very attached to the rhythm parts on the songs I write. And Andrea [Whitt] and I are playing as a duo now too. We call our genre Acid Americana. I play some resonator guitar in that project, which is kind of like an old dobro but with a normal neck. The body is made out of metal or it has a metal cone on it so it resonates. It's a blues guitar thing. It has a really nice warm sound. We're inspired by more stripped-down sounds like The Wood Brothers, which is one of my favorite bands out there now.

Does Katie & Andrea just perform Grateful Dead music?

No. Our relationship came out of the Grateful Dead, but we just released a new EP of our own stuff. We're actually booking a lot of shows where we're playing our original music now. It's really cool because during the Dead & Company tour we had to take a lot of Grateful Dead songs that we learned [for the pre-show VIP Loose Lucy's Lounge performances] and learn how to make them work as a duo, to strip them down to the song itself. It was huge in terms of helping us discover how to arrange our own music. It allowed us to see that we could cover a lot of parts by doing it our own way. It's easy when you just have two people in a room making the decisions. We're very excited about it. But prepping for that helped us learn how to create our original work.

(Katie Skene and Andrea Whitt comprise the duo Katie & Andrea. Rich Saputo.)

When did you first see a Dead-related band?

I wasn't around for the actual Grateful Dead. I was too young. But amazingly enough the first two times I saw anyone from the Dead, was when I was playing with them, which is insane. My first real experience with members of the group came about through The David Nelson Band, who I had been sitting in with and working with a bit. They had heard my EP and I had met them at the Nelson Family

Vineyards when they invited me to open up for them as a solo act. At the end of my set, Nelson and Barry [Sless] and Pete [Sears] and Mookie [Siegel] came onstage and we played a few songs, some Blind Faith, some Freddie King and Delbert McClinton, "Two More Bottles of Wine." We jammed on those and it was fun and then I hung around for the David Nelson set and after that we started talking about putting together a band [California Kind] with Rob Barraco. A couple months later David Nelson fell and broke his shoulder and then he was diagnosed with colon cancer, so they had to fill in without canceling a bunch of shows and they asked me to help out. The first one we wound up doing with Peter Rowan, but they also had an annual show booked up in Alaska. Then Bob Weir heard that David was sick and decided to help out. The promoter in Alaska was thrilled. This was basically a sports bar that they play up there and now Weir was going to jump in.

When was this?

This was in March of 2017. So Bobby comes up and and we're all there and I was insanely nervous. I was so young. We basically would do a set as California Kind where we'd play about five songs and then Bobby would come out and play solo and then everybody would go up and play, and as the nights went on I would get up and sing backup and harmonies. It was actually my first Dead experience. It was a crazy three nights playing with Weir. It was a crash- course in how the Deadhead world goes. I was in over my head. I'd been to some festivals where the Allman Brothers had played before, but I wasn't aware of the whole cover band world that had spun off of the Dead. My next experience was a while later when I wound up playing with Phil Lesh. But the first time I got to see any iteration of the Dead, without being involved with playing, was this past fall when I went and saw the Wolf Brothers. That's when we started talking about doing the whole thing with Steve Parish, which led up to touring with Dead & Company last summer [2019]. It's been a whirlwind.

Do you have any thoughts about the popularity of Grateful Dead cover bands, or bands that have jumped on the Dead bandwagon? Is it overkill?

It's hard to say. Whenever you're creating music that makes you happy and serves your truth I think it's amazing. And you know there appears to be an audience for bands that can capture that spirit. Personally, I don't feel fulfilled by playing only covers. I love playing some choice covers, but I get the most out of playing original music. And I'm going to play my song right because I wrote it. So automatically the way I play it is right. The pressure that comes from some Deadheads can make me a little nervous because they can be very critical. But there's nothing wrong with making music you love if people seem to like it. That's all you can hope for. Plus a whole new younger audience has been turned onto it. So whatever keeps the spirit giving works. You'll even hear bands that play primarily original music working Dead covers into their sets. I think it's amazing. It's like the gift that keeps on giving. There's no wrong way to honor the Dead.

What do you do for gear? I saw that you have a nice Gibson SG that you play?

Yeah, so I've had that SG since I was about seventeen. I actually bought it from Rick Lollar, who is another friend from Tallahassee. He plays with Jimmy Herring. And then I have another SG that I keep in open E. It's actually John Molo's guitar. Those are my main guitars that I take around with me and I'd like to eventually supplement them with a [Gibson] 335, but I haven't gotten there yet. I have an old fifties Kay Pro that I don't like to take on the road very much, but it's a cool sound. It has kind of a Jimmy Reed vibe to it. And I have an Epiphone Masterbilt that I've been playing a lot lately now that I do more acoustic things. When I went out with Steve Parish I played his custom-made Alvarez. They made one for him and one for Jerry in 1993 I think it was. It's beautiful. It sounds incredible. I don't know all the specifics. It's a gorgeous guitar. And mostly I play out of a Blues Deluxe amp with a tweed cover that I've had forever.

Have you switched out the speaker or are you using the stock Fender speaker that came with it?

I use the original speaker. I've had it for so long that I've gotten used to it and I've dialed in my sound around it. My pedalboard is pretty minimal. I have a CryBaby wah, and I have a Keeley Katana clean boost which I love. And I recently got a BB Preamp which is an overdrive by Xotic pedals that I used for the Dead & Company tour. I love it. You can get a lot of different sounds from it. I also have an Aqua-Puss delay that I occasionally use to get a more washed-out sound. It's like a spacey delay. I also have a tremolo pedal that I'm using. I forget what brand it it. Andrea loaned it to me. That's pretty much it for me. I'm always been a fan of Derek Trucks and Duane Allman. You know if you can make it sound good just plugging in and playing and using your own fingers without getting too complicated. I'm a fan of that. I've always preferred it that way. I try not to rely too much on technology.

Did you get to know John Mayer during the Dead & Company tour?

Yeah, we talked to him a little during the tour. He was very kind and generous and he's a big fan of Steve Parish. They did an interview together. I really enjoy his approach to what they're doing. I think it's cool to have someone in the band who's an artist in their own right and a songwriter. And obviously you have to be a kick-ass guitar player to be able to fill that role. You know Jerry was so into originality and being an original player. I think he would think it's really cool that someone with their own voice who has influenced so many people would pay so much respect and homage to this catalog.

(John Kadlecik. Ardmore Music Hall. 2019. Photo by David Tracer.)

John Kadlecik

Considered to be one of Jerry's most convincing emulators, John Kadlecik took his Garcia tribute to new heights in the years after the Grateful Dead stopped touring. One of the founders of Dark Star Orchestra and a member of several top-tier Jerry Garcia- and Grateful Dead- related acts, including Furthur, with former members of the Grateful Dead, and the Golden Gate Wingmen, Kadlecik echoes ol' Jer like few others. Whether he's delivering a spot-on version of "Lazy River Road," venturing into Garcia-inspired takes of his own material or rendering a spirited cover of a rock classic, Kadlecik brings a welcome authenticity to his playing.

Where'd you grow up?

I was born in Iowa and I grew up around the Midwest, in Ohio and a few places. My dad was a city manager, so we'd move about every three to five years. But before starting high school I landed in a suburb of the Chicago area and that's where I started planting roots as a musician, when I was about thirteen.

How did your musical journey begin?

I taught myself to read music when I was around seven. I was enchanted by the sound of the violin and the cello. We had a babysitter that practiced cello and I was sort of a Beatles nerd. The string sounds on a lot of those Beatles tracks caught my ear. So I chose the violin as an instrument to play. In fourth grade the kids at my school were all given a listening test to see if they could tell what pitches were higher and lower and I was able to do that easily so I just kind of took it from there. As a a freshman in high school I auditioned to be third chair of the high school orchestra, which is kind of like stepping onto the varsity football team as a backup quarterback. Eventually I lost interest in it and got more interested in musical improvisation, so I taught myself how to play guitar.

Did you start out on an acoustic or go straight to the electric?

I started out on acoustic guitar because it was a loaner. My dad was out of town for a convention or something and I was staying at a friend's house for a week. My friend was a year older than I was and he had a guitar and a Mel Bay guitar instruction book. I kinda just flipped through the book and learned some chords and stuff. By the end of the week I'd pretty much gone through the whole book. Then my friend said, "Hey do you wanna just keep borrowing the guitar for a while?" So he let me borrow it and later my mom ended up getting me an electric guitar and an amp for my fifteenth birthday.

Were you the only musician in the family?

My mom was a visual artist. She lived in Cincinnati, and I'd go down there quite a bit, but I was the only musician in the family. So there wasn't a lot of direct musical influence from my family other than getting a few Beatles albums handed down. I had started out on the violin, but eventually I got into rock and started listening to Rush, Black Sabbath and Led Zeppelin. I played hard rock for a while in the eighties. At my first public show I think we played some Ozzy, some Cars, Chuck Berry and Jimi Hendrix. Stuff like that.

How'd you arrive at the Grateful Dead?

The drummer that I played with a lot turned me onto them and I listened to albums like *Mars Hotel* and *Europe'72* during my first semester of college. At the time I was studying jazz and trying to invent a kind of New Age dance music with an edge to it. Then I went and saw the Grateful Dead play and I was like "Oh that's what they do!" I had seen some of their graphics and some transcriptions of "Casey Jones" in a guitar magazine but even though I had played stuff like "Purple Haze" before I wasn't generally into songs that seemed like drug songs. I thought the Dead were going to be more like biker music, like Motörhead or something, and when I finally got turned onto them I went, "Wow, this is the heart of American music. This is the best of it all."

What was your first time seeing the Grateful Dead?

Well my first attempt as seeing them was during the summer of 1988 in Alpine Valley. I figured I'd just go up there and try to get a ticket. Communication wasn't as great back then as it is now and I didn't know that it was sold out so I drove up. I didn't get to see them that summer, although I had fun roaming the parking lot and checking out the scene. Back then you didn't have to pay for parking and everyone parked in these big fields. I finally got to see them perform in the spring of 1989 at the Rosemont Horizon, on the the third night of their run there. It was great. They were still kicking ass and having collective peaks together, much as they had in earlier eras. After that I wound up taking in about fifty Grateful Dead shows while Jerry was still alive and about fifteen Jerry Garcia Band shows. I also saw some of the early RatDog shows when they were just an opening duo on the JGB tour.

Did you have a big moment when you decided you wanted to play in the style of Jerry?

Well, I was already in a place where anything that I liked and wanted to listen to more than once, I would gravitate to wanting to play it. When it's what my heart wants, my fingers follow. Like I said, I was in the process of trying to invent Grateful Dead music when I stumbled upon it. I was trying to create something that was spiritual and that also had the fire and passion of Led Zeppelin along with a dance groove that pulled it all together. I'd thought the Dead were just some classic rock band but when I saw them I realized they were completely cutting edge. It wasn't nostalgia. It was about people getting into it and it was happening right in the moment. It was like this crazy underground thing that I had no idea was going on and when I found it I couldn't believe it. It was incredible. It was like going through the looking glass or through the wardrobe you know? I didn't go to shows to sit and stare at Jerry. I danced and had fun and got into a joyous state. I would gravitate to right in front of the soundboard where I though the sound was best. I appreciated Bobby and the other members as much as Jerry.

How do you feel about trying to achieve a sound that's close to what Garcia did?

When I played in my earlier bands we didn't lock it into character. I might play the Bob licks on the chorus and the Jerry licks on the verse and I would trade off with the other guitar player. By the time I saw my first Dead show I had already been in two bands and I was starting to learn how to manage and lead groups. I'd also been in the studio and had taught myself multi-track recording. I was starting to study jazz and consider ethnomusicology as an academic path. So I already had a bit of a knack for playing the guitar in a way that is similar to what an impressionist does with vocals.

What were some of your early Dead-related bands?

(John Kadlecik. Furthur. Broomfield. 2010. David Tracer.)

I played in a band in Chicago called Hairball Willie, which shared some early jam roots with groups including the Deadbeats. These were bands that came out of this guy Frank's basement. He was a puppeteer on the Ren Faire circuit. I came into Hairball Willie as a replacement for the original guitar player in 1991. Before that I had been in a band called Uncle Buffalo's Urban Mountain Review, which got a mention in *Relix* all the way back in 1990. We had a regular Friday night gig where I got to polish my chops and out of that I auditioned for Hairball Willie. In Hairball Willie I had a repertoire of about thirty original tunes by 1995. Our release [*Just Defying Gravity*] is still out there on CD Baby. Eventually I started to dabble in the notion that maybe I should just go ahead and let some of the stuff I learned from Jerry leak into my other music and not just contain it to Grateful Dead songs. At some point all the influences start to leak out and into one another.

(John Kadlecik. Quixote's. Denver. 2015. D. Tracer.)

How'd you get to DSO (Dark Star Orchestra)?

It started as a notion I had for Hairball Willie as a special event. As a fun thing, we played a Grateful Dead set list from an old show and had a contest for people who could guess what the show date was. One of the things we realized was that it's really hard to find a Grateful Dead set list that we knew all the songs to, and we wound up just doing a second set and I think we were still a couple tunes short. I was looking at the book *Deadbase* and I thought that for the right band of Deadheads it would be a cool project to pick shows and learn all the songs from those shows. So after trying it out once with Hairball Willie I thought about putting together a best-of-the-Chicago-area Grateful Dead players band and doing the guess-the-show thing. I thought we might play once a year, but as it came together in the summer of 1997 we got a regular Tuesday night gig at a place called Martyrs' and it started to take off. Hairball Willie had wrapped up and I'd just quit playing with a group called Uncle John's Band and I was back to doing my own original project which I was calling Wingnut at that point. We started out with plans to play about eight shows and move on, but by our sixth show we were pretty much sold out. The original keyboard player, Scott Larned, had plans to move to Oregon, but he changed his mind. So Scott stayed and we started doing the occasional weekend shows and then we got asked to do an all-ages theater show by a big promoter in town, Jam Productions, at the Park West. After that we got calls to play in New York and then we got booked at the Fillmore in San Francisco. That was only like a year-and-a-half after we formed. It was a really good band. We had all done time in our own original groups but we had also all played in Dead cover bands and we were all Deadheads.

When did you stop playing with DSO?

I stopped playing with them in 2009 when Furthur formed.

How was it making the transition from covering the Dead's music to actually playing with some of the original members?

Well, I was collaborating with them. I figured there's a lot to learn here but at the same time I was like, "Eh, I know a few tricks." There's a lot of ways to come to this music. And I had to deal with the baggage of some of the people who had come before that really had nothing to do with me. But it was a really fun run and the thing I'd most like to point out about Furthur was the amount of new material we worked up. What I really liked was that immediately after forming we started working on "Welcome to the Dance," which was a new Phil song. By a couple years in we had almost an album's worth of new songs that we played.

Did you know most of the songs that Furthur played from having spent time in your previous Dead cover bands?

Yeah, I once put together a list of all the people I've played Grateful Dead music with and it was seriously more than a hundred people.

How many years were you in Furthur?

For about four-and-a-half years. We toured pretty much the same amount as the Dead did. We were doing sixty to seventy shows a year. We did a spring tour, a summer tour and a fall tour. It was like drinking out of the firehose. We did a lot tunes. I mean there were only a few tunes that I never played in DSO and we got to those in Furthur. And we covered some random new stuff, like "Train in Vain" by the Clash and I talked them into a George Harrison tune called "Any Road." And the Ryan Adam's tune "Magnolia Mountain."

I enjoy your Jerry-inspired guitar tone and I really appreciate your singing voice. Does your voice just happen to sound like Jerry or do you work on that?

Well, my voice tends to sound like what I hear in my head. I have a really good memory for melodic fragments. When I was a violinist I committed to memory the entire first violin part of Beethoven's Fifth Symphony. So I can handle a certain degree of difficulty. At a young age I found that I could do an impression thing. In DSO I was in character as Jerry and I was just singing Jerry's parts. There's a melodic DNA to it. There's a true melody and then there's a way that the melody can be pushed and pulled around in different ways. I know the phrasing and I think that's all it takes for a listener. Everyone listens actively. It's a scientific thing.

Are you a gear-head in terms of chasing the Jerry tone?

For me it's been more about my approach than about my equipment, though sometimes equipment helps. I didn't have a big budget for gear in high school. I'd gotten a nice start from my mom with a guitar and a cheap amp but it was more about struggling to get what I could with the pay that I got working a part-time job at a library. I think I got pretty close without exactly cloning the gear. I guess I could say that one of the first times that I tried to apply the Jerry sound to another song was on the first Hairball Willie record on a song called "3 a.m.," which is a good example of getting a tone that's pretty close but with just my own gear. And then when DSO started I didn't want to go for the gear initially, but I'm an electronics geek so it was a good excuse to learn more about tube amps and tube preamp design. Basically what Jerry did was he started with Fender Twins and then they made his Fender Twins as clean as possible with the highest quality capacitors and the best preamp tubes you could get and then they tried swapping out the power amp section with high-grade linear power amps and then they started into the Wall of Sound thing where Jerry's amp went to the sky. Before that point Jerry wasn't usually in the PA. They would put a mic on his amp for recording purposes, but generally they would pretty much stack as many twins as was needed for the space. If it was a thousand-people room, we need four twins, or if it's five thousand people, we need eight twins, or whatever. With the Wall of Sound they built the cabinets very precisely so they could stack them safely ten or fifteen high. They had everybody set up that way, including Phil. And when they got done with the Wall of Sound, Jerry just kept the bottom four speakers of it for his amp. They kept using that. There were a few other experiments, like in '75/'76 he was playing some Mesa Boogies instead of Fender Twins. I gradually sort of modeled the sound, and stumbled on little things that would refine it – like the JBL speakers, which give more headroom and a wider frequency response. It's a high-powered speaker that's not meant to break up like a Celestion or a Jensen. They aren't meant to give character. JBLs are meant to reproduce. Jerry wasn't the only guy into JBLs. Duane Allman was way into them for his sound and Clapton was into it for a while.

How do you feel about the proliferation of Dead music?

I think of it as a whole scene like reggae or bluegrass. It's gone beyond a band and into a whole genre onto itself. Making music is a human birthright and in this day and age, after radio, TV and then the Internet, the notion of trying to be original is really hard. But the possibility of being authentic is as simple as choosing it. That's what I try to tap into. And it's good to try and be original but not to the exclusion of making music that serves the community.

On JK's Jerry-related gear:

I go for the basic pedals and at this point I've expanded on them. I've put a micro-synth in with the octave pedal so it does the octave plus a whole bunch of cool shit that I can dial in with it. The MXR Phase 100 is definitely a cool phaser and a distinctive Garcia phaser sound. I've tried to use some digital algorithms to emulate it, but nothing gets it exactly on, it's a unique unit. I have a vintage Mutron III, which is in my big rack that's stored in San Francisco, and I have several guitars including a couple PRS EGs, a Carvin, an early eighties Vantage VA-800 and my Alembic Orion with a cocobolo top, walnut body, a five-piece maple and purpleheart neck with flame maple sides, an ebony fretboard and a knobby peg-head.

(Halina Janusz. San Luis Obispo. 2020. Photo by Hal Masonberg.)

Halina Janusz

The daughter of a pioneer of the Southern California sixties folk scene, Halina Janusz didn't learn of the Grateful Dead and Jerry Garcia until she attended a Quaker camp in her teens. With a powerful voice and a charismatic persona, Janusz is a key figure in the band Jerry's Middle Finger and in the Southern California jam scene in general.

Did you grow up in California?

Yes, I was born in Southern California, and I moved up and down the state a few times. I grew up in the Los Angeles area, where my dad was a well-known folk singer. So I came up around a lot of musicians and rehearsals in our living room at night and all kinds of interesting instruments and music from all over the world. My dad's name was Michael Janusz, he passed away in 1981 when I was younger, but he was a mover and a shaker here on the folk scene in L.A. He was sort of a regular at a club called the Ash Grove, which was a famous venue. My dad would pack the place for a week or two straight. He had lots of fans here. He influenced a lot of younger artists, including people like David Lindley and the band Kaleidoscope. He passed away before he was able to fulfill all his musical dreams, but he was a hell of a singer and the founding member of a group called the Westwind International Folk Ensemble, which was an influential folk group that played at the Monterey Folk Festival. He was truly an under-the-current force.

So how'd you get to Jerry and the Dead?

Interestingly, it ties into when my father was ill. He had a degenerative brain disease. It was a very dark time. It took quite a while for him to pass. It was very difficult to watch him go from a brilliantly talented man to someone who had little capacity to even speak. I watched him forget songs and so on. It was a tragic time for me, because the light in our world revolved around him and all the stuff he had going on. When I was nine we moved up to Central California. My mom got a job directing a Head Start program and we relocated. My dad would travel back down to Los Angeles for gigs and stuff. But when he got sick and was in the hospital, I was kind of a wreck and I needed to get out of the area for a break. In the summer of 1980, when I was fifteen, I found an awesome Quaker work camp near Santa Cruz, where there were some cool rustic people, including a lot of hippies and some very down-to-earth folks involved in the Quaker community. I'm not particularly religious. I grew up Russian Jewish on one side and Polish Catholic on the other. But I went off to this Quaker work camp in Ben Lomond, California, and there were these super cool chicks from New York there who were traveling and they came to the camp for a few weeks. They were really into the Dead and Neil Young and there I was pretty green with my banjo and I was jamming with one of them who was a musician and she turned me onto the music.

She was like, "Ok, you've really got to listen to Garcia." We went to a record shop in Santa Cruz one day and she started pulling out vinyl and was like," Ok, you need this and you need this, and pulled out the albums *What A Long Strange Trip It's Been* and *Workingman's Dead*, which I bought new, and a couple Neil Young albums and stuff like that. This was in a time when I was in this really funky place in my life. I grew up in L.A. and now I was living in a cowtown, where I'd met these cool chicks. It was an eye-opener for me. I had heard the name Grateful Dead but I thought it was hard rock, and then I discovered it was music that was right up my alley. I was in a dark place and all of a sudden this light was shone. I went home thinking, "Hey, I've got a lot more living to do and there's stuff I can explore." The Grateful Dead brought a lot of that to me. It was a healing force.

When did you get to your first Dead show?

My first show was in 1983 at the Greek Theatre in Berkeley. After the Quaker camp I went up to a Quaker school in Grass Valley, CA, where we all lived in cabins. It was another cool experience, and I ended up at my first dead show out of the experience

Did you ever get to see the Jerry Garcia Band?

Yeah a few times. I saw Jerry acoustic in 1983 in Grass Valley. I think David Grisman was there too. There was a reunion of The Band too. I was probably in altered states.

What was it about Jerry's sound that hit you?

I think I would say it was probably the improvisational jamming that got to me. I'd never really heard music go off like that. I'd grown up going to classical concerts and folk shows and I'd been to a couple of rock concerts, but not many. I think that's what it was. And I'd grown up on so many different types of music. I liked hearing ouds and tablas and a wide variety of Middle Eastern instruments. I'd heard all these exotic sounds growing up and my dad playing everything from Janis Joplin to Arabic vocal music or Russian Gypsy music. Jerry and the Dead offered up so many different sounds. It appealed to me. And the structures of their songs tripped me out. Like "St. Stephen." It wasn't what I was used to hearing on the radio. It was a whole new language. Their chord progressions were similar to some of the folk songs I knew but they would take strange and unpredictable turns. The landscapes that the lyrics would paint were also very intriguing to me. First it was the sound of the music and the extemporaneous quality of the musicianship. It was unique and I was drawn in. And then it was also the people. It might actually have even been the people first. Those awesome girls who turned me onto it. If not for them I might never have sat down and listened to the music.

You play a few different instruments right?

Yeah, I've studied a bunch of instruments. But banjo and guitar are the ones that stuck with me. Probably because I can accompany my voice with those. I taught myself guitar and I took banjo lessons for years. I play clawhammer style, kind of like Neil Young plays banjo or Abigail Washburn, who is a clawhammer- and frailing-style banjo player. I've played in a bunch of projects where I used the banjo but I also play guitar and I'm a songwriter. I have a jamband called Mother Jones that's been around for a long time. It's on hiatus right now because I've been so busy with Jerry's Middle Finger. We have three albums of stuff that we've done. I work with Son Vo in that band, who was also the bassist in JMF for the last few years before Burt Lewis. He's moved on to work on some original stuff, but Son, Lisa [Malsberger] and I go way back.

(Left to right: Garrett, Lisa and Halina at Skull & Roses Festival. 2019. Photo by Rich Saputo.)

Have you ever sat in with Melvin Seals and JGB?

Lisa and I got to sit in with Melvin and JGB for the first time last December. I think it was 12.18.18 at the Merry Jerry Christmas in Pomona. We were asked to sit in along with Oteil [Burbridge] and John

Kadlecik, which was a big moment for us. JMF was arriving in a big way. We had a bunch of friends and family at the show who had no idea that we were going to join the band. It was all of our local people. They were screaming our names. We had a blast. It's on Archive. It was so much fun. That kicked things up for JMF even more. As the two women in the band who get to do that, it was great. We get a lot of love and respect from our guys. We're not just backup singers in the band, we're full-fledged members of the group. It's a six-person team. We all wear a lot of different hats.

We all bring things into the band. It's important to me. I've fronted bands before. I'm a teacher and I do music programs all over Southern California, so I'm comfortable on the mic. Lisa and I are two very strong women. Some might call us forces of nature. It's nice to be working with a group of men who really respect what we bring. I've sung with bands where I was just the "chick singer," but that's not the case here. It's not easy for women to earn respect in this scene. Lisa and I are right out front. We're not standing in back by the drums. They initially put us right out front and that's where we've always been. We bring an element that the audience connects with. All the years I've been seeing JGB the ladies have been in back, but when we did the Merry Jerry Christmas the producer put us right out front. It was cool to be out front with Oteil and John K. Once they heard us start singing they both pointed to the sound guy to turn us up in their monitors. That let me know we were on the right track. Oteil had this big smile and his shoulders were up and he closed his eyes while we were singing. I was like, "Ok, we're doing this right!"

Did you study the JGB backing singers?

Yes. After Donna Godchaux and Maria Muldaur, who sang in the earliest version of JGB, the original singers were Jackie LaBranch and Gloria Jones. Gloria passed away last year. And one of the other singers that came in, I think while Jerry was still alive, was Shirley Starks. After Jerry passed she brought in Cheryl Rucker who was part of the [post-Jerry] era of JGB. We studied both eras of singers, and we know a few different versions of backing vocals that we do from the different eras and Lisa and I like to throw in a couple of our own little things too. We try to stay true to the original arrangements but on a couple songs we add a little something of our own, but you have to know the music real well to know what they are. We've even seen people in the audience watching us intently on this intricate part of a song and a couple guys were waiting for it and they knew what the part was and when we did it they smiled and high-fived each other and went "They did it!" That's how intense the music is for the fans, and that's how much we want to bring them what it is they need from the music. People come up to us and say things like "I'd thought I'd never ever hear that again." Garrett has studied the hell out of Garcia. We're an ensemble crew.

Have you always enjoyed the styles of music from which JGB draws?

I grew up listening to a lot of gospel. My dad used to listen to a lot of Southern gospel. That seeped into my style. Lisa and I both have power in our singing. When we did Skull & Roses Festival last year we were standing there watching Melvin [with JGB] and we noticed that they brought the ladies up front, for the first time ever. Maybe Melvin realized how much the audience responds to the women vocalists being out front and possibly made the changes based on that. Melvin's comment to Garrett was "Those ladies sound real good."

I've been singing in Dead bands and Jerry bands here in Southern California since the early nineties. There were bands here that were doing Dead music when I first moved back from Northern California. A good friend of mine, Chuck Berez, who is a well-known California Deadhead, introduced me to all these musicians who were playing this music in Southern California. So I went from being a fan in Northern California to meeting Chuck who introduced me to these musicians who were actually playing the music. That's how I really started playing the music of the Dead. A couple of the guys that I met through Chuck asked me to do some backup singing with them. Bands like Stunt Road, which is still around but it's a totally different band now, but we packed venues in the West Valley every Thursday night with like 150 people.

How do you feel about all the bands that play Dead music these days?

I think it's cool. Going to what I was just saying to you, I've been in a couple of these local, fun bands. There's a boom right now with this music. I don't know if it's because of Mayer or because of weed culture or what, but we have eighteen-year-old fans coming to our shows knowing all the words to songs, and not just Dead songs but JGB songs! It's blowing my mind. It was the little bands here in L.A., like the Purple Turtles, Stunt Road, and The Rum Runners that helped push the music out there. Some of these musicians overlapped with Cubensis, which is a band a lot of Deadheads know. It's a lot of the same guys who circulate between the bands. I think that this is what happens in a lot of areas. I don't think that Bobby and the guys would still be doing what they're doing now if it weren't for all the baby bands in the cities and towns and villages keeping the music going in the bars, clubs and coffee houses. These little bands keep the music alive, just playing Grateful Dead music to their hearts' content. This might be the most important component in why the scene is still thriving—these hard-working groups that stick to it.

(Steve Kimock. Petaluma. 2016. Photo by David Tracer.)

Steve Kimock

Steve Kimock came into a wider public view when Jerry Garcia referred to him (in a 1988 *Guitar Player Magazine* interview) as his favorite unknown guitarist. His musical career took hold in the seventies, eighties and nineties in San Francisco, where listeners appreciated his work with the band Zero and other groups (The Goodman Brothers, The Underdogs, the Heart of Gold Band with Keith & Donna Jean Godchaux, KVHW) and relished his occasional sit-ins with other Bay Area jammerati — not to mention his work on the road with The Other Ones, Steve Kimock Crazy Engine and RatDog. Kimock is clever and inventive in his approach and remains his own artist while also being a regular contributor to various Dead-related projects.

You played with Jerry when he was alive, which makes you one of the ground zero musicians among those who play music that takes some of its influence from him . . .

Yeah, he and I were a lot alike on a basic level. We were both guitar geeks and self-taught players. He was one of those guys that never quit practicing and I was like that too. It's a guitar thing. If you practice a lot and you play all day every day you start to see some kind of progress. I never got the impression that he could walk away from it. Even though you might wind up getting into very different stuff over time you never really get off that track.

Were you a big fan of Jerry's music when you were younger?

When I moved to Northern California in the seventies, which was in the shadow of the Dead thing, I played pedal steel and I was a big fan of electric blues, so I was coming from a lot of the same places in terms of influence that Garcia was. He had more of a bluegrass background than I did and I had more of a jazz influence, but when I got to California people would [listen to me] and say "Oh you sound like Jerry Garcia." I was trying to sound like Roy Buchanan, but I had the wrong guitar (laughs). If I'd had a Telecaster maybe I would have sounded more like Buchanan and nobody would have compared me with the Dead. It wasn't like I was that into their music or really wanted to play it, but because of peer pressure or because there was an audience for it or something, I sort of got into it. I was a Bay Area musician and there was overlap between the local artists. I remember getting gigs for my band Zero in San Francisco, which was hard enough, and there would be absolutely nobody in the room and then I'd go outside and there'd be this giant crowd beating down the door to get into the venue a few doors down, because Jerry was playing.

I preferred to have my own thing, but I was also playing a bit with Keith and Donna and doing the Kingfish stuff with Weir, which I didn't mind obviously, but I tried to keep my own identity.

How old were you when you first got into playing the guitar?

I got a guitar when I was in junior high school, and by the time I was sixteen I was playing with a drummer who I liked to jam with, and I thought, "Yeah, you know I'd really like to do this." I had a flash that if I didn't do anything else, I could have fun with the guitar. And so I pursued it.

So you weren't a huge Deadhead . . .

Not really, some of my friends and bandmates [Billy and Frank Goodman] were. They were scaling walls to get into shows back in the day. They would crawl through the ventilation ducts to get in (laughs). They were old school East Coast Deadheads. But I was into different stuff, although I really appreciated Jerry's influences and playing. When *Europe '72* came out and I heard it I was like "Holy shit this guy's fucking good!" Even though I was into different stuff, I began to understand how very sophisticated and attractive Jerry's music was.

(Kimock with Prang. February 2017. Photo by David Tracer.)

Did you get to check out a few Dead shows?

Oh yeah, the first time I went was with a friend of mine, Michael Bendinelli, who was the chief tech at Mesa Boogie. We went to Winterland. Mike was a good guy and my best friend back in the day. He was a super cool dude and he knew all about the Grateful Dead. He had all the tapes and stuff. I wasn't hip to the whole bootleg thing, but I'd drive around in his car with him and he'd play these live Dead tapes from the one-drummer era where the music was just so elegant. You know, like Weir's cowboy shit and these really extraordinarily well-played, great- sounding recordings with these super-creative, absolutely no-fucks-given straight-ahead jams. I heard it and I was like, "Yeah I see what this is about." I loved it but I didn't try to do it. I would try and do Dickey Betts stuff or Eric Clapton but I didn't try to do [what the Dead were doing].

Did you get to hang out backstage with Jerry and company at all?

Yeah, a few times. I went to the Warfield with Donna during the acoustic shows that they were doing there [in 1980]. I also went to the Henry J. Kaiser when Jerry did his return after his coma [in 1986]. Is spite of the fact that he had just been on death's door Jerry played and sounded great. I got to hang out with him for that. I played with his guitars and tried to provide emotional support. I also hung out with the band one year in New York before he played Madison Square Garden. So, yeah, I hung out back-stage a few times . . . but the Dead's crew wasn't really like, "Hey kids come on back and hang out with Jerry Garcia!" (laughs). They'd look at me kind of like, "What's this guy doing here?!" Whether you were in the band or not you sort of had to be careful where you stepped.

So you weren't attending Dead shows and dancing around and so on?

Not really. My overlap was that I was a Bay Area musician. It was more of a local music community thing. What I loved about San Francisco back in the day was the variety of players and the really unique stylists everywhere you turned. John Cipollina was in town. Mike Bloomfield was there. Terry Haggerty. George Van Eps was up in Santa Rosa. Joe Pass was in town for a while. Bill Kirchen of Commander Cody. Freddie Roulette. Albert Collins. Ali Akbar Khan for crying out loud. The Rowan brothers. Grisman. So many great string players right there. David Nelson. It was really just amazing. Part of what was cool about the whole thing was that at a certain level people were used to the idea that the guitar could sound different and so there was very little that was cookie-cutter about anything. It was really neat. Great great players and everyone playing on the same scene. It was wonderful playing with all the people that those cats played with, like John Kahn and Merl Saunders and Nicky Hopkins and Bill Vitt. We were all Bay Area musicians. I might have been at the tail end of it a bit, but I don't have any problem identifying myself as a Bay Area psychedelic guitarist. That's where I cut my teeth.

Now that the music has gone wider and the psychedelic jam thing has gone beyond the Bay Area . . . how do you feel about the artists who continue to play in that tradition?

Well, I don't really go to those kinds of shows normally. Sometimes at a festival I'll hear another band doing that and sometimes it's pretty fuckin' cool. Especially if the people have been at it for a while.

Someone like Melvin [Seals] always has a good band. And if you're at a party on a beach somewhere and Dark Star [Orchestra] is playing and you hear it from a distance, it's just perfect.

What do you make of the enduring popularity of the Dead's music?

Well, if you did the Venn diagram thing, with the Grateful Dead being the center circle, every other band would overlap with that circle, not the other way around. There are ways that people listen to music, where they know the songs, but they don't know if the drums are playing the right thing and they don't care about the hi-hat or whatever. They don't really give a shit. It can have nothing to do with Jerry Garcia at the level that the music is consumed by the individual. In music cognition there are presumed listening modes that include sing-along listening, nostalgic listening, ecstatic trance where everyone in spinning together, etc. There are all kinds of ways that the music is used. People go to that book, or to that energy, to gather and understand things that might not have anything to do with the guitar. As a trained listener you're listening for cues or similarities to other pieces of music. You know that the experience that you're having is not the experience that other people are having. The Dead were just playing their own music and then all these people adored it. But people approach it differently. I think that Jerry Garcia was concerned with his legacy. I think he actually thought about it in terms of being an improviser. Garcia needed the tunes. He needed the book to be the point in a way. The music itself was worthy of study.

Do you enjoy working Dead music into your sets?

Yeah to some degree. I do an ensemble thing and I leave space for that. In SKB we played a lot of math rock and we had complicated crazy modern electronic stuff going on and then someone would shout "Play some Robert Hunter songs." And I'd be like "That's not what's happening here." But I love "Crazy Fingers" or an instrumental version of "Stella Blue." I don't feel weird covering the Jerry stuff instrumentally. But when you start to sing it or copy it then I think inevitably people start making comparisons.

Do you think there are too many Dead cover bands? Has it been done to death?

Well there are market forces at work. I'm guessing there wouldn't be so many bands if people didn't want to hear that music.

Or could it be that there are lots of people who want to play the music because it's fun?

I hadn't thought about that, but at that level, yeah go for it. I studied it pretty deeply to play with members of the band, so I didn't want to fuck it up, but if people play it because they love to get together and have a band, and there's safety in numbers or whatever, I can only look at that and encourage it. Please play music. Get together, smoke a joint and throw off the cares of the world and know yourself better, but on the other end of it, if you played something and I was like, "Dude that's supposed to be an A7 not an E chord . . ." well. But yeah I think it's cool. Personally, I'd get a little tired of it. I got asked to do a lot of it for a while and everyone was kind of playing the same songs. Having done it with Phil and Bobby, it made it hard to understand the point. It felt watered-down. It was turning into ritual. The whole point of being able to do it is that the experience is authentic. Everything about it is felt. If it becomes musical auto-pilot, no thanks. Because I remember a time when it wasn't like that. There were a lot of diverse acts back in the day. After Jerry died, it was like okay we have to play his music. But you know play your own music too.

Do you do anything special with your pedals when and if you're going for a Garcia tone?

I'll use a little reverb pedal or an echo pedal or some kind of fuzz box, or some modulation if I'm covering Jerry, like a phaser or a Uni-Vibe to give it a little twist. Even though I have a giant pile of electronic stuff that I enjoy tinkering with to create specific applications, for me it's really about using as little as possible. For the most part, Jerry got solid, consistent and high-quality tone out of his guitars. He could get just as much out of a Strat. If there's a lesson in all of this I think it's that one important thing that the Dead did was to use a dynamic map, where they played the verses at one level and the other parts at another level. They had a real clear idea of when to play loud and when to play soft. They had a basic roadmap where you state an idea, take it for a drive trough the trees, build it to a crescendo, climax and then you're done.

How do you feel about musicians who try to emulate Garcia and the Dead?

It's superficial, but at the same time I've heard people who can really get it note-for-note. Some people think that what Jerry did was super delicate but he played with a lot of force and a lot of volume. A lot of the cats who emulate him get into first or second gear, but nobody really opens it up the way he did. As far as trying to replicate it, I'd rather be thrown into a wood-chipper.

Set Break

(John Mayer and Bob Weir bring new life to the old book in Dead & Company.
November 2015. Photo by David Tracer.)

Road Tripping with Nick Paumgarten

In the summer of 1986, aged seventeen, I was freshly blessed with a driver's license and thus the newfound means and liberty to follow the Grateful Dead. Two friends and I conspired to cross the country and intersect with the band at Ventura. Late one balmy night, we drove the trip's final leg from Las Vegas toward the coast – *Fear and Loathing* in reverse. No ether or mescaline, but we had a few other things. We were somewhere around Barstow when the desire for a burger took hold. We rolled into a Denny's. The counterman asked where we were from and where we were headed. We giddily announced that we were going to see the Grateful Dead. "Didn't you hear?" he said. "Jerry Garcia is in a coma." He had to be messing with us. This was, of course, pre-Internet and pre-iPhone. The best you could do was turn on a radio and wait for the news. Queasily skeptical, no longer giddy, we got back on the road to Ventura and pulled into the Fairgrounds at first light. There were maybe a couple dozen vehicles in the lot and a ragged assembly of forlorn enthusiasts still awake, observing a whacked-out vigil. The news was true. The shows were canceled. Jerry was in a diabetic coma. What now?

This first intimation of absence, the abrupt silencing of the Tiger, was a shock to many systems—the band, the business, the touring circus—but it was principally a blow to our yearning ears and souls. I was a few years into the obsession, had collected dozens of tapes and heard dozens more, and had seen a bunch of shows, but in spite of witnessing Garcia at his unhealthiest (him singing about death while looking like it), I'd never really considered the possibility that the music might ever stop — that there'd be an end to new notes or that the world would be deprived of the sound of his guitar.

We all know what happened next: Garcia recovered, the band flourished, and we got nine more years, many of them good ones. But for a while we weren't sure. That same summer of 1986, I returned to the East Coast and became a regular at a bar in Merrick, Long Island, called the Right Track Inn, where a Grateful Dead tribute band called the Volunteers performed every Saturday night. The group had a bearded lead guitarist named Jeff Mattson, who proceeded to blow our teenaged minds. They played a lot of stuff that had fallen out of the Dead's mid-eighties rotation, and they played it in the style we'd heard on old tapes and records. One night, the bouncer, realizing our I.D.s were fake, turned us away. We hung out on the sidewalk outside and listened through the vents to a "Dark Star" that brought to mind bootlegs we had of the Dead in Europe from 1972.

Mattson, who went on to anchor the Zen Tricksters and later the Dark Star Orchestra, is an excellent artist in his own right, steeped in jazz, Motown, and gospel. But I'd be lying if I didn't say that what drew me to him was the way he played like Jerry—he'd listened closely and had achieved a fluency that allowed him to express himself in the idiom without coming off as a slavish imitator.

In the years to come, and especially after Jerry's death, I encountered more and more Garcia interpreters and inheritors —some reluctant, some unabashed. Some dedicated to achieving the exact approach of this or that year, others inspired by the songbook and the improvisational latitude to forge phrasings and even songs of their own. Some listeners and critics look down their noses at the imitators, while others, jonesing for their Jerry fix, pine for nothing more (or less). I'm not here to say which is better or cooler. Originality is of course the coin of the realm, and anxiety accompanies influence, but art is also theft, imitation is flattery, and Jerry is Jerry, and for those who simply love his approach to music—his taste, his tone, his sense of melody, rhythm, and dynamics, his imagination, his generosity, his restraint—who can begrudge them the conjuring of joy?!

Even the surviving members of the Grateful Dead have wavered in their preference, sometimes opting for more of a sound-alike, other times reaching for new sensibilities. In their various configurations and new collaborations, they've invited some of the best pickers out there to fill that hole, either to introduce their own inimitable styles to the mix or to have a go at sounding like Jerry. Personally, I dig it all, even if I dig some more than others. The Garcia vernacular makes for a fascinating line of inquiry, an ever-renewable resource, an ongoing conversation and argument, and as often as not an exhilarating and soul-stirring night out. Thirty-five years later, I still go to see Mattson whenever I can, as well as many of the players who are interviewed in this volume, and many who are not. I write this in the midst of the long Covid-19 lockdown, and there is perhaps nothing I miss more than live encounters with these artists—and the sound of the thunder with the rain falling down.

— Nick Paumgarten
New York City, NY
April, 2020

Nick Paumgarten is a staff writer at the *New Yorker*.

(Above: Melvin Seals takes the crowd to church. Skull & Roses. Photo by Rich Saputo.)

(Right: Warren Haynes channels Jerry on Garcia's original Wolf. Rich Saputo.)

(JRAD, Joe Russo's Almost Dead, brings the music to the next generation. Broomfield, CO. 2017. Photo by David Tracer.)

(Golden Gate Wingmen. September 2018. Great American Music Hall. SF. David Tracer.)

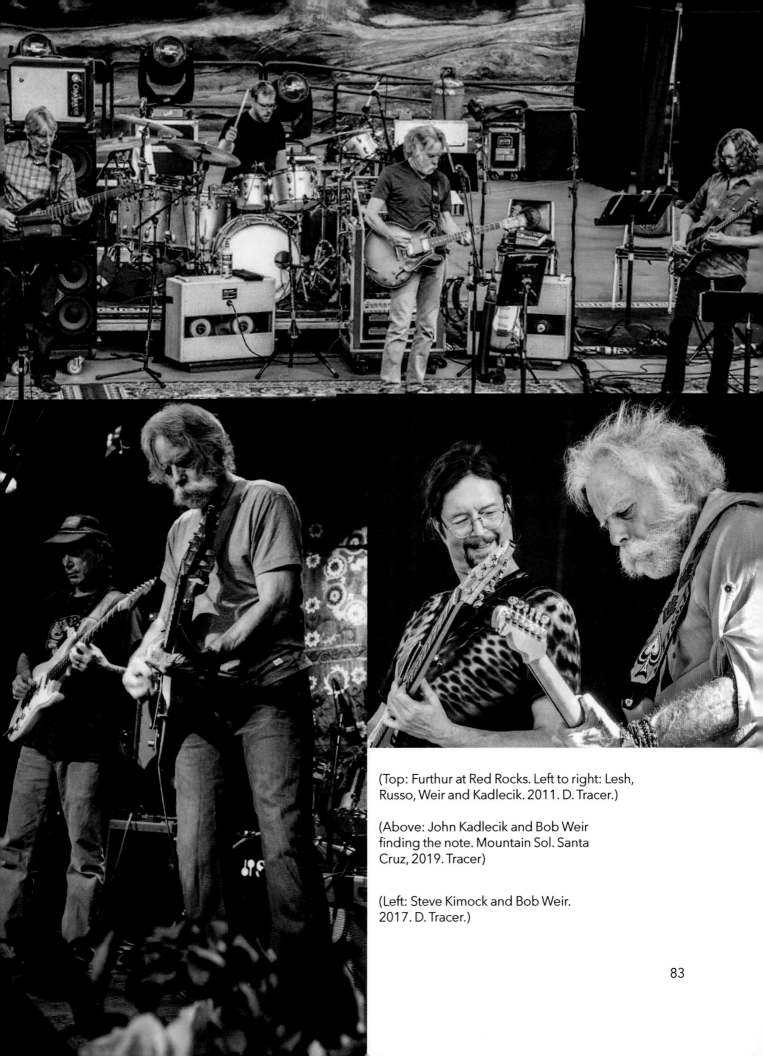

(Top: Furthur at Red Rocks. Left to right: Lesh, Russo, Weir and Kadlecik. 2011. D. Tracer.)

(Above: John Kadlecik and Bob Weir finding the note. Mountain Sol. Santa Cruz, 2019. Tracer)

(Left: Steve Kimock and Bob Weir. 2017. D. Tracer.)

83

(Lisa Malsberger. Skull & Roses Festival. 2019. Photo by Hal Masonberg.)

Lisa Malsberger

As a vocalist in Jerry's Middle Finger, Lisa Malsberger brings a welcome bit of SoCal edge to the soothing tones associated with JGB's gospel-, blues- and r&b-tinged catalog. Malsberger uses the music as a kind of medicine in her life, finding peace and spiritual solace through her performances with the group. This interview occurred on the day of JMF's show at the Sweetwater in Mill Valley on the twenty-fourth anniversary of Jerry's passing (August 9, 2019).

Am I correct in thinking that you have a day job as a dental hygienist?

Yes that is correct. My license plate reads: ROCKNDH. It has a double meaning: it means the "Rockin' Dental hygienist" and it means the "Rockin' Deadhead." I've always been a Deadhead, but I'm a little bit hippie and a little bit hood.

Where are you from originally?

Well I was born in Inglewood, California, but I moved around a lot as a child. My dad was a dentist in the army. We landed in Texas when he left the service and then he married our next door neighbor. So my mom and my sisters and I moved back to California when I was in middle school. After that I lived with my single mom for a while. She passed away in July of 1995 just a little over a month before Jerry died. It was one hell of a few weeks. I was nineteen at the time. I think like all my bandmates I was a really unusual kid. I grew up for a few years in the South Bay around a lot of snotty kids and I was this t-shirt, jeans and skateboarding Deadhead chick who liked the Beastie Boys and Metallica and all kinds of other stuff. I was also really into JGB. I always loved those ladies singing.

Do you have kids?

I do, I have three kids. Two girls and a boy. They're twelve, ten and eight.

Wow, you must be pretty busy with your job, your kids and the gigging . . .

I am, but I absolutely love it. It's a really good life. With Jerry's Middle Finger everything has come full circle. For years and years the Jerry Garcia Band was my crutch. In the late nineties and early two-thousands I was one of the original members of The Makers, which was a JGB tribute band in Southern California. Part of that experience was that I actually got to play a full show with Gloria Jones [of the Jerry Garcia Band] in San Rafael. When she first got to the gig she just kinda looked at all of us. We were a motley crew I guess. I was this young white chick that she couldn't make much sense of at first. She was very gracious like she always was, but I could tell she was a little apprehensive, kind of like "Okay who is this girl?!" We started with "How Sweet It Is," and during the solo she pulled me back off the mic and gave me this biggest giant hug and said, "Oh my god you're such a surprise."

How old were you when you first started checking out Jerry and the Dead?

It's a long back-story, but when I was a young kid I stuttered horribly, which held me back academically. And one day this lovely lady came into the counseling office at school. I think I was in third grade at the time. She was a hippie-trippy little lady who had a Stealie patch on her purse. She interviewed me and talked to my parents and she wound up telling my parents, "I think your daughter needs a creative outlet because she's highly intelligent and could be skipped ahead." I stuttered so hard that I didn't want to read out loud and my childhood was kind of stressful. So I started singing gospel music in a choir as therapy and I stopped stuttering. That really built my love for gospel. But that one lady with the Stealie on her purse helped to heighten my senses and as I got older I really started liking the Grateful Dead. As I got to know more about what Jerry did I discovered that he was singing with these gospel singers in JGB and that was it. I'm kind of getting choked up talking about the moment I found JGB. I mean look at me now. I just got a message from Cheryl Rucker, former backup singer for JGB, saying "You guys are all the talk of San Francisco right now and we can't wait to be there for a show." We've been trying to get her out for a show. I've got all of Jerry's old singers talking to me. It's blowing my mind. These ladies sang me through years of grief and they didn't know it, but now here they are accessible to me. It's incredible.

Who are the backing singers from JGB that everyone should know?

So, there's Gloria Jones, who recently passed away, and Jacklyn LaBranch and theres Cheryl Rucker and Shirley Starks. Those are the two primary pairs that I have spent years listening to and years being influenced by. Since Jerry passed away Melvin has toured with many different formations of singers and players, but those were the singers who toured with Jerry. I've immersed myself in all the JGB music. The cadence of Jerry's voice singing with those gospel singers is like medicine to my soul. Period. Our band, Jerry's Middle Finger, concentrates on how to recreate that feel.

Did you ever get to see the Grateful Dead or the Jerry Garcia Band?

I went to one Dead show when I was nineteen years old. It was in 1992 the year after I graduated from high school. I also made it to one Jerry Garcia Band show that same year at a venue in Redondo Beach. I wish I had been a little older so I could have been on the tour circuit with those bands. My real union with the Grateful scene started in about 1999 when I moved to San Pedro and started singing with The Makers. But I've been listening to the music for a long time. I've watched so many videos and listened to so many hours of Garcia Band and I've studied them so much that I feel like I was always there. But I only had the honor of attending one Dead show and one JGB show and then I started singing the music.

Do you have a particular approach to singing the Jerry Band material or do you try to replicate a specific backing vocalist from JGB?

Well, singing was used as a therapy to help me stop stuttering, so it's a comfort for me and it's something I've always done. I don't really approach it with any special kind of style. I make sure I'm in the right key of course, but I just love the music. To me, singing is just like walking. I approach it like I would anything. I feel really lucky to be able to do this. I get so lost in my head when I'm singing the music. A lot of people have told me that they like to watch me sing. They say "Man watching you sing makes me feel better." Hearing that from people makes my heart swell because that's how I feel. Sometimes we'll be performing a song and someone will start to play a solo and I'll look out and see this big crowd and everyone's light is shining and I'm like "Holy crap we're doing this." We put it out there and they give it right back.

Are there any tunes from the Jerry Band repertoire that really get you?

I really love "Gomorrah" and I love singing "Lucky Old Sun," "Dear Prudence," "Shining Star," "I Shall be Released," and I really like "Mighty High." That one just lifts me off the ground. I get goosebumps all over my body when I sing these songs.

Do you do anything technical with the tone of your voice?

I'm pretty much just singing the music. Halina has this incredibly beautiful voice, whether she's going high or low, and our voices just work together like magic. She and I had jammed with the guys [in Jerry's Middle Finger] by ourselves a few times and when we finally all played together we looked at each other and went "Okay, we're never not doing this without each other again." We're not copying anything, we're stepping up as ourselves to pay tribute to people who have been so inspiring to us. You can't overthink it, this comes from the gut.

Do you listen to any of the newer school Dead-influenced bands?

I've listened to JRAD. They're cool. I'm also good friends with the guys in Cubensis, who are a great Dead cover band from Southern California. I also like Lightning Dan and the Crawdads; and Miracle Ticket, which is a big Arizona band.

Did you have a particular moment when Garcia's sound really hit you?

Well I'd always loved the Dead but especially JGB. After my mother died in 1995 I really leaned on the music and after I got out of my first marriage, which was crappy, and when I first moved to San Pedro, I became friends with this husband-and-wife couple from Croatia, Pete and Ljil Mazich. Pete played organ in The Makers and his wife sang in the band.When Ljil got pregnant I got the chance to step into the band and fill in. My real aha moment was when we did the show in San Rafael with Gloria Jones. After we played the gig Gloria bought me a Cadillac margarita and we sat there talking. She shared some personal stuff with me. She told me that she had to stop touring with JGB so she could be a full-time parent to her grandchildren who needed help at the time. I was really touched that she was being so open with me. Here I was in my twenties, drinking this margarita with one of my idols and she laced her fingers in mine and said "You have the voice of an angel." That was a pretty overwhelming moment. I cried the whole way home. Gloria Jones is my reason for making it through this scene and finding my way. Music has been a powerful force in my life.

(Jeff Mattson. Dark Star Orchestra. Boston. 2018. Photo by JD Cohen.)

Jeff Mattson

E very now and then you might luck out and find yourself at a small venue listening to an incredible musician putting on a display of true talent for a fortunate handful of audience members. Such was the case when I saw Jeff Mattson perform with Donna Jean Godchaux's band. Perhaps best known for his lead guitar role in the Dark Star Orchestra, the former Zen Trickster captured the unwavering attention of a small audience at an intimate bar in Denver with his impressive guitar wizardry on a simple Stratocaster. From that point on I was hooked. Mattson conjures the best of what I liked about Garcia — blistering and inventive solos that come straight from the heart and soul.

I read somewhere that your dad is a jazz musician . . .

Yeah, I grew up hearing a lot of jazz from my dad. He's retired from playing now, but he performed all around New York City and on Long Island. He still plays around the house, but for my whole life that was the sound of being at home. He was either playing it or listening to it on his record player.

Was the guitar your first instrument?

My dad, being a practical person, suggested I should play bass when I first started. He said I'd get more gigs that way because there was a need for skilled bassists and there are tons of guitarists. So I played the bass for about a year and I enjoyed it but I soon realized that I would have more fun playing lead guitar and soloing. So when I decided that playing lead was what I really wanted to pursue I switched over. My dad supported my decision.

Did you start listening to the Dead via their albums?

Yeah, initially in the early seventies I first heard *American Beauty* and *Workingman's Dead*. And then I bought *Skull & Roses* (1971) and *Europe '72*. Those live records were what really turned me onto them. I liked the studio stuff too but when I heard their live sound I was really blown away by it. And then when I saw them actually perform live and saw how they jammed and how they played fresh stuff every night that was it for me. Maybe it was because of my jazz influence. It really excited me.

Did you try to replicate Jerry's playing?

When I started out playing I was more interested in getting the essence of what they did and how they got there and then I sort of interpreted it for myself. There's nothing wrong with the approach of learning stuff note-for-note though. I had a friend who I played with for years who when he was eight years old learned every note of the Allman Brothers' *Live at Fillmore East* album. To this day he can play along with that entire recording. That's an encyclopedia of blues and jamming right there. I took a different approach though, which seemed more logical to me.

Did you ever get a chance to meet Jerry?

Yes, once in 1993. I was with some people who were staying at the Ritz Carlton in New York City and the Dead were in town for some shows. Jerry was hanging out at the hotel bar there and he was chatting with some young girl. When the girl got up to go to the bathroom, my friend, who was bolder than I was, introduced herself to Jerry. So we got to speak to him for a few minutes. I had just heard them play the song "The Days Between" for the first time the night before and I told him that I was really blown away by it. It must have been the right thing to say because he was excited by that and he said that he was really happy how the song was turning out. It was just a nice moment. I don't keep a journal but when I went home I decided that I should write it down to remember it. It was a significant experience for me.

When did you first see the Dead play live?

My first show was in September of 1973 at the Nassau Coliseum. It was the first time they played the full "Weather Report Suite." I also remember that they played the Keith Godchaux song "Let Me Sing Your Blues Away."

Did you consider yourself a Deadhead as a teenager?

Oh yeah, I lived and breathed the Grateful Dead. I went through that obsessive phase where it's all I wanted to listen to. As the years went on I got back into listening to other music. I think the Dead served as a catalyst that made me want to listen to the stuff that had influenced them. Now I have a huge collection of music. It spans just about every kind of genre there is. I have a voracious hunger to hear music of all types.

What are you listening to at the moment?

Let's see, I'm just looking at the pile on the table in front of me. I've got some Dylan, some Van Morrison, some Neil Young and some Wilco, but also some Sun Ra, Stan Getz, Bach, Nick Drake, Morphine, the Residents, Ginger Baker, Richard Thompson. That's just what's in front of me.

Do you think that the music of Jerry and the Dead has been reinvented in any way since Jerry died?

I played three shows with Phil Lesh & Friends in the fall of 1999. I knew every note Jerry played and all of that, but Phil was really interested in taking the songs to a different place, more like rearranging them. It took me a little while, because I have a taste for the original stuff, but I got what they wanted to do. With bands like The Other Ones they were trying do stuff that was a little different. The feeling was that no one was going to replace Jerry because he was such a unique player and that he couldn't be replicated. Later with Furthur and Johk Kadlecik, who was really schooled in Jerry's style, it was different, but when I played with Phil at those shows they wanted to play the repertoire and jam of course but they also wanted to take it to a new place. It makes sense in retrospect. RatDog did that too. They wanted to make the music their own. Even with Dead & Company they do some stuff their own way, but it's also kind of gone back a bit to the original approach too. So they push the envelope for a few years and then they pull it back a little bit I guess. It moves around.

How'd you fall in with DSO?

My band the Zen Tricksters had done a lot of shows with them and we hung out with them. They knew us and we knew them. And Rob Barraco, who was in the Tricksters, filled in for keys when their keyboardist [Scott Larned] passed away. So that was a direct connection for me. And I also knew their sound engineer well who I had worked with.

Can you share a bit about your gear?

I have several different guitars that address different eras. These guitars are wired and electronically set up like Jerry's guitar but they aren't Tiger copies or anything like that. I never really was drawn to replicating the exact gear. But when I joined Dark Star it became evident that it was an important part of the gig, so the [guitar collector] Andy Logan asked me at Red Rocks if I would be interested in playing his Tiger copy that Leo Elliott built for him. I said "Sure bring it and let me play it." We did two nights at the Boulder Theater in Colorado. I would never have known that it wasn't the original. I enjoyed it. And I've also played Wolf a couple times in the Boston area. I just saw that they are auctioning off Alligator [Jerry's vintage Stratocaster that he received as a gift from Graham Nash].

Do you try to copy Jerry's tone with your gear?

I don't feel bound to copy Jerry's exact tones or notes even. I have other guitar influences. When I perform with DSO I have to pay a little more attention to play something that's not necessarily what Jerry played but what he might have done. I'm sure I'm totally influenced by him in my playing but I don't feel compelled to edit other stuff out. When I do gigs with other projects I just use a simple combo amp and a Strat with some pedals. In that setting I'm not concerned with replicating the gear.

I'm not dissing anyone, but all the electronics in the world and the right pick and the rights strings are only gonna get you so far. The actual playing should be the most important thing. But if you're a weekend player and you have some money, the one thing you do have control over is getting all the gear, so I can see that.

Are there too many Dead offshoot bands now?

Well ultimately that's what's going to keep it alive. When I was in my first Dead cover band in the mid-seventies there weren't that many Dead cover bands. It was an insular scene for people in the know and the rest of the world was sort of oblivious to it. The idea of tribute bands wasn't what it is now. It's changed over the years. But here we are twenty-five years out and wow there are more than there ever were. I think part of it is that people are largely just waking up to how great this music is to play. And bands like The National or whoever have discovered the Dead. It no longer has to be their dirty little secret. It resonates with the alternative scene now. Which is great. It's all good. That's what keeps it going. In DSO we fill a niche for people who want to hear it like it was played back in the day. You also have Phil & Friends, Dead & Company, the Wolf Brothers and band like JRAD who go in their own direction. But there's a place for people who want to hear what it sounded like back when it was first being played. We don't really "copy" it. We have all studied it quite a bit. All the eras of Dead music. It's kind of scholarly. We're not doing anything radically different than anyone else. The idea that we copy a show note-for-note is kind of laughable. It would take me months to learn how to play just one show. It would be Herculean task.If you are at all aware of the mechanics that would go into doing that you'd realize that it's almost impossible. Plus that's not at all what the spirt of the Grateful Dead is about. If we're doing a '73 show it will sound like a '73 show, because we play the set list, or we include a particular jam that they did on a certain night that we might want to pay homage to, but it's not going to be exactly what they did. We do an elective set list every third or fourth night on the road where we select the tunes we want to play. People are divided about that. But hey, you pay the money you takes your chances.

What guitars do you play?

My guitar is a Warmouth Guitar that Brad Sarno put together for me when I first joined DSO. It's basically a Stratocaster but it has a Warmouth body and neck. It's got some cool stuff built into it that enables me to get the essential Jerry tones, plus the effects loop and a special pickup that allows me to do the synth guitar stuff from the nineties era. I have another stock Strat that was modified by Brad Sarno that I use for the '72 -'74 era. Then I have two Travis Beans. I have one that was made about four or five years ago. It's a replica. They made ten of them that are like the Travis Beans that Jerry played in '77. And in '76 Jerry played a stock Travis Bean. I have one of those too. And for the '69-'71 era I have a D'Angelico guitar that sounds like Jerry's Gibson SG sound on *Live Dead*.

How long do you think you will keep doing this?

I don't have an end date. I'm 61 now. As long as it's fun and I'm physically capable, I'll be playing.

(Stephen Inglis. Waʻahila Ridge State Park. Honolulu, HI. 2019. Marlowe Holt.)

Stephen Inglis

Stephen Inglis is a Grammy-nominated guitarist who was born and raised in Hawaii. Among other projects, he formed the group House of Spirits (in 1998) with legendary Grateful Dead drummer Bill Kreutzmann. In 2012, Inglis's duet album with Hawaiian music legend Dennis Kamakahi, *Waimaka Helelei*, won a Na Hoku Hanohano Award, Hawaii's highest musical honor. In addition to his interest in traditional Hawaiian music, Inglis is a creative innovator and has recorded three releases of his own singer-songwriter material and a 2018 album, Cut The Dead Some Slack, which interprets Grateful Dead music in the slack key style. Inglis fronts his electric band, the Stephen Inglis Project, blending original material with the Dead, Dylan, Hawaiian music and more— he is also a member of the Grateful Dead-inspired acoustic trio, Fragile Thunder, with David Gans and Anela Lauren.

Where are you living these days Stephen?

I live in Honolulu, which is where I was born and raised.

When did you first start playing?

I started out playing classical piano when I was five years old and then I became a member of the Honolulu Boys Choir between the ages of seven and nine. The choir was an early introduction to the world of music performance. We did lots of high-profile performances and traveled to places including Taiwan and Guam as well as playing around Hawaii. I picked up the electric guitar when I was about fourteen. Then one day when I was around sixteen my older brother and I dropped some acid and listened to *Led Zeppelin IV* and the live Grateful Dead CD *Without A Net*. Like a lot of people, I had heard "Casey Jones," "Sugar Magnolia," and "Truckin' " on the radio but didn't really get it until I heard that live stuff. The mind-expanding sacrament also helped.

Did you ever see Jerry or the Dead live?

My first shows were at the Shoreline Amphitheatre in 1993. I actually made it to sixteen Grateful Dead shows, which was kind of tricky to do living in Hawaii. I was happy to get there at the tail-end of Jerry's career for sure. It blows my mind to see some of the dedicated young kids who are just diving into his music now and never got to see him play. His legacy is incredible.

Is there a big Deadhead community in Hawaii?

Not a huge number but there are some.

You have some background playing the music of the Dead right?

Yeah, from 1998 to 2001 I played with House of Spirits, with [Grateful Dead drummer and Kauai resident] Bill Kreutzmann. It was the thrill of a lifetime. We played around Hawaii. A little after that I moved to San Francisco for a bit, where I kind of got homesick and decided to start playing the traditional music that I had grown up with. That's when I started to focus on playing slack key and traditional Hawaiian music. I put out an album in 2011 called *Slackin' on Dylan*, which eventually led to releasing *Cut The Dead Some Slack* (2018). So I started out as an electric guitarist and came to the acoustic stuff later. A happy cosmic event occurred when I was at NAMM [National Association of Music Merchants] in 2016 in L.A. I was playing a Hawaiian tune and this haole guy walks up and he's singing along. I kind of recognized him. It was Blair Jackson. He was the editor of *Acoustic Guitar Magazine* [and the author of *Garcia: An American Life* (1999)]. It turned out that he was a longtime slack key and Hawaiian music fan. I was a fan of his work having devoured copies of *The Golden Road* and *Dupree's Diamond News* as a youngster. He had sent me a long email in which he praised my Dylan release, and in which he had urged me to cover the Dead in the same style, but I never got the note. It must have gone to my spam box. So, our conversation [at NAMM] wound up being the genesis of *Cut the Dead Some Slack*. Blair hooked me up with David Gans, who I eventually started collaborating with via computer and who I asked to lend some vocal harmonies to my stuff. David came to Honolulu in 2017 and we played our first shows together.

Can you tell me a little bit about slack key?

It's an acoustic guitar tradition that started after a group of Mexican cowboys came to Hawaii in 1820 to help control feral cattle on the island. The vaqueros would rope cows all day and then at night they'd sit around the campfires and play. The music started with the guitars that they brought to the island and their unique open-tunings, which evoke the landscape of the islands. They left the guitars on the island as gifts and the native Hawaiians developed a style of playing them. Slack key is a fingerpicking style, where the key is "slacked" or the pitch is brought down from standard pitch a little, but when people hear "slack key" they are probably thinking of Hawaiian steel guitar which is played with a bar. A young Hawaiian kid named Joseph Kekuku invented the steel cylinder and the way of playing with raised strings on the lap. This went on to have a huge impact on twentieth century American music. The lap steel helped give birth to the electric guitar and the pedal steel. As the Hawaiians traveled, they began bringing home all of the wonderful sounds that they were hearing: delta blues, early jazz, ragtime and a lot of beautiful cross-pollination. These styles borrow from each other. The raised-slide lap style collided with the Hawaiian style, etc. There was lots of cross-pollination as lap steel collided with mainland music. If Garcia would have chosen to pick up Hawaiian style slack key it would have been beautiful. Just the way he used space and phrasing, like the way he interpreted old Jimmie Rogers songs, I think he would have likely fallen right into that sweet spot

Are there certain Dead songs that lend themselves more to slack key playing?

Yeah, it was a fascinating process of figuring that out. Obviously, I wanted to retain the element of the Hawaiian sound. And so I had to find the right songs. Anyone familiar with the Dead catalog is going to be aware that something like "Brokedown Palace" is going to lend itself more easily to slack than say "Victim or the Crime." The Hunter/Garcia ballads are good for it as far as songwriting style. They had a more traditional way of writing I guess one could say. "Cassidy" ended up being the only Weir choice. I wanted to keep it in the Dead spirit though, so we stretched out on a few of the tunes. "Days Between" is on the album. That goes back to when I first started hanging out with Bill Kreutzmann. It just worked. I get goosebumps every time we play that one.

Do you still play electric Dead music?

Yeah, in the Stephen Inglis Project we do all kinds of stuff. I've played at Terrapin Crossroads about five times now with some great players including Mark Karan, Robyn Sylvester and Danny Eisenberg. Every time I jam with them it's amazingly fun. It's been great to get back to playing jamband stuff as well as doing the slack key and acoustic material. I started playing with Gans in 2017 and then we started Fragile Thunder with Anela Lauren, who lived in Hawaii for a while. She lives in Colorado now. She recorded a project called *Harpin' on the Dead* that I played on. I knew her from when she used to come to see my band Palolo Jones. Palolo is a valley in Honolulu. We played some Dead in that band.

What are your thoughts about the extended Dead music scene these days and how the music is being reinterpreted and re-styled?

Well, it's amazing how the whole scene has grown with DSO and JRAD and bands that take it in other directions like Shred is Dead. Joe Craven and the Sometimers is another group that really takes it out stylistically too. What they do live is so original and so good and so natural, even though they're pushing the boundaries, it's not contrived. It's not a novelty. It just flows.

(Left to right: Stephen Inglis, Anela Lauren and David Gans are Fragile Thunder. Photo by Rita Hurault.)

Do you get into any of the Jerry gear in terms of guitars and pedals?

I don't have a Tiger or a Wolf. Those are amazing, but those aren't really my niche. I soaked up my style by listening to Jerry. I'm a musical omnivore and I'm a completist, so I'll go all the way down the rabbit hole if I really like something. What Garcia did with his on-board effects loop (OBEL) was brilliant; the more pedals you put in your chain the more it sucks your tone, so Jerry was able to keep his pure tone, even with all his effects. The two cables in his OBEL setup enabled him to send a pure pickup-to-amp signal and let the level of all of his effects stay even. I achieve a similar thing on my rig with a Friedman Buffer Bay unit. I makes a big difference when I use it. And Garcia used a Boss overdrive, but I favor a Strymon. They're able to grab an amazing analog vibe that simulates the kind of high gain that you would usually get from an amp. I'm stoked with my rig right now. Gear is a slippery slope for guitar geeks. I get into it but I try not to add too much too often because when I make changes it takes time to work it in. I play Lowden guitars from Northern Ireland. I've been playing those since 1997, when I bought my first used one from a friend. They're beautiful handmade instruments. I eventually met the Lowden people at NAMM in 2011 and I got endorsed by them. For slack key I play a bigger-body one. The whole neck looks skeletal and like its warping side-to-side, almost like your tripping. They have these special frets (fan frets) that give you great bass and really clear treble. The bass has more growl and the highs are more bell-like. John Mayer has a Lowden that he really likes. Ed Sheeran plays them too. My electric one, which is a GL-10 model, has a koa wood body. It's my main electric guitar. I love it. It just sings. It got a beautiful flame top. The wood is from Hawaii. Koa only grows here. It's great tone wood and it's pretty rare, though now they're working on making it more sustainable.

(Anela Lauren with Celtic harp. Photo by Kent Kobakoff.)

Anela Lauren

Jerry Garcia's music takes its listeners on journeys. Some would say it's capable of transporting them to astral planes and beyond. Enter harpist Anela Lauren, whose Garcia-inspired plucking on the Celtic harp facilitates such trips to the other side. Lauren comprises one-third of the acoustic trio Fragile Thunder with David Gans and Stephen Inglis.

So you live in Colorado now?

Yeah I moved to the town of Lyons a few years ago.

How did you come to fall in with the group Fragile Thunder?

I knew Stephen [Inglis] from the nineties when I attended The University of Hawaii and my friends and I used to go see his band Palolo Jones play at Anna Bananas in Honolulu every Friday night. Later on I moved to Kauai and started playing the harp. I made an album [in 2013] called *Harpin' on the Dead* and I asked Stephen if he would play on it. He hadn't been playing the Dead that much at that point. He'd gotten into playing slack key guitar a lot, so I take credit for helping pull him back into the Dead world. When I sent that album out for promotion, David [Gans] picked it up right away and started playing it on his radio show [The Grateful Dead Hour] and then I met Gans at the Gathering of the Vibes. I had my little harp with me and he had his guitar and we played a live set together there which aired on his show. After that we started playing gigs whenever we could. Then separately, Stephen started playing with David and because we all knew each other we figured we should just all play together.

How'd you first get into the Dead?

During my high school years someone dragged me to a show one summer. And from the moment that everyone started singing all together I was hooked.

Where'd you grow up?

I grew up in New York.

Where did you attend your first Dead show?

It was in Pittsburgh at Three Rivers Stadium in 1986. I was taking a summer course at Carnegie Mellon University and I went to the show with a group of people. Then later when I went back to college at Wesleyan University in Connecticut, we'd drive down to Madison Square Garden for runs of Dead shows in New York City.

Were you a musician from early on?

Yeah, I grew up playing the piano and taking classical piano lessons for eleven years. Then I stopped for a while. In college I got into jazz and improvisational music. They had a great world music program at Wesleyan and I took a year of jazz improv from a fantastic vibraphonist named Jay Hoggard. He got me interested in playing music again.

Did you play in a band at that point?

I joined my first band was when I was living on Kauai. I'd been playing the harp for a while and I was playing for weddings and meditation and yoga and spiritual healing stuff. I formed a group called Lilia with some folks there. I played with a woman called Cindy Combs. She's also known as the Slack Key Lady. It was sort of jazzy and lounge-y.

So you'd been into the Dead for quite a while . . .

I think I saw about eighty-plus Grateful Dead shows and about fifteen Jerry Band shows before moving to Hawaii. I did come back to the mainland for the 1995 summer tour. I caught all of that except for the last two shows. The scene had changed a lot since 1993, but I had a really fun ride.

Can you explain how you approach the harp when playing Dead music?

Well the song "Ripple" came naturally because of "the harp unstrung" part of it, plus it's a cool song. So that one had been on rotation for me before I ever played with other people. During the process of making *Harpin' on the Dead* I went through the Grateful Dead song book and discovered that most of the songs that worked with the harp were Hunter/Garcia tunes. There are a few Weir tunes like "Cassidy" and "Black Throated Wind" that work too. But the harp is a very ethereal instrument so it can get you in touch with other worlds and dimensions. I sort of play it in Jerry's honor.

Is it challenging to play with other people on the harp?

In a band, the harp kind of takes the place of a keyboard. It's very similar in terms of where it sits in the mix with the highs and lows. The vibration can be in that same angelic place that a keyboard can occupy. It's strong but it's also very delicate. I try to fit in with bands but I can get overpowered by the drums and a lot of times the guitarists will turn up really loud, so I so I have to be kinda picky about who I play with.

I like the sound of Fragile Thunder, which is a perfect name for that group by the way. It's strong music music but it's also delicate. You all seem to listen and allow space for each other without overpowering one another . . .

Yeah, David calls our band a democracy.

Your singing on "Must Have Been the Roses," which I heard on a live recording of Fragile Thunder, sounds great . . .

Thanks, that one is right in my range. By the way, I have a couple stories about channeling Jerry. After I made *Harpin' On the Dead*, Jerry came to me in a dream, right as I was waking up one day. He told me that he liked my version of "Attics of My Life," that was on the release. That's my first story. The second one was when I was trying to get tickets for the Grateful Dead50 shows in Chicago. It was really hard because so many people were trying and trying and I had put in for a three-day pass after getting kicked out of the ticketing system a couple times. So I finally put down my phone and lay down on my bed when I got a visitation from my dead mother and then a visitation from Jerry. I sat up and looked at my phone and there was a text that read "How would you like to pay?" It was a miracle. I got a three-day pass for two hundred dollars from Ticket Master.

Can you tell me a little about your gear?

I play a Celtic harp, which is different than the pedal harps that are used in orchestras. On all harps, the strings are laid out like the white keys on a piano. There are levers at the top of each string which shorten the string half a note, producing sharps. On a Celtic, or lever harp, you sharp each string by hand. On a pedal harp, you use your feet to make those adjustments. I've got a pickup stuffed inside the sound box, which sounds better than just putting a microphone in there.

Do you run your harp through any pedals?

I pretty much like a good clean sound, but I'm looking at maybe using a flanger or a delay. I might also like some kind of wah-wah for tunes like "Fire on the Mountain" or "Dark Star." I think that would be really fun.

What do you think about all the artists out there playing Dead these days?

I think the more Grateful Dead the better, and I also think the more creativity the better. I'm more of a JRAD person than say Dark Star Orchestra. I think if you're gonna cover something it's gotta be either different or better. And I don't see how you're going to make it better, so I'd go with different. I'm certainly not gonna knock anyone for playing the Grateful Dead though. You can't go wrong.

(Tyler Grant. Photo by David Tracer.)

Tyler Grant

As a bluegrass flatpicking guitar champion and a highly regarded player in the jamgrass community, including a well-acclaimed stint in the Emmitt-Nershi Band, Tyler Grant knows his way around roots music. Grant is a longtime fan of Garcia and the Dead, with a keen interest in the music of Old & In the Way and all the bluegrass associations that flow from that side of Jerry's background. He fronts the group Grant Farm and teaches flatpicking and bluegrass guitar among other pursuits.

Where'd you grow up and did you come from a musical household?

I grew up in Jamul, California, in East San Diego County. My dad, who was from Texas, was our camp-fire entertainer. He played guitar and sang early popular songs by Johnny Cash, Elvis Presley and Carl Perkins. My parents are both music lovers and we listened to music all the time on the home stereo and in the car. My father would make mixed tapes. He famously said that he, "Dropped out of rock and roll when Elvis joined the Army." So we listened to a lot of country and Americana music, mainly from Neo-traditionalist artists like Ricky Skaggs and Emmylou Harris. We had plenty of sixties rock and folk-rock albums from Creedence Clearwater Revival to Cat Stevens but we never listened to the Dead and I was not familiar with their music until my late teens.

How'd you come to learn about the Dead?

I learned about the Grateful Dead in a unique way. My parents told me that my dad, as an undergrad at Stanford University in the mid-sixties, had taken guitar lessons from Jerry Garcia, who was teaching at Dana Morgan Music at the time. I remember my mother explaining, "He went on to start a band called the Grateful Dead who people follow around the country." My dad said, "He wasn't a great teacher, he just wanted to play all the time."

Once I got into the Dead, I would try to influence my father to like them. He would resist, saying, in reference to the instrumental jams, "It's all one chord. They never change chords!" I finally got him into the *American Beauty* album, and he learned all the words to "Ripple," which we sang together from then on. He loved "Ripple," and associated it with his second wife who died from breast cancer in 2002. My step-siblings and I sang it at her funeral. Once my father softened to Dead music, he would joke and say "I taught him that lick," when the music played in the background. This is all part of a cosmic connection that I have to Garcia. My father did not remember too many details about his handful of guitar lessons, but I have to believe that Jerry played his guitar, a 1964 Gibson B25 that my dad bought new, and which was my primary guitar for my first eight years of playing. I also believe that my dad must have sung one of his classic Carl Perkins songs for Jerry, which Jerry might have noodled over. I have this idea that Jerry totally dug my soulful little dad from Texas who sang great and had solid rhythm. I have met one other man who studied with Jerry at that time as a young Stanford student, and he remembers more details about the music store and the lesson studio, which was upstairs around back. This fellow, Bob Fisher, says he was the last student of the day on Wednesdays. After the lessons, Garcia would be picked up by his wife and the couple would sometimes invite Bob to go to the movies with them.

What instrument did you first start to play?

My mom and dad made my sister and me learn piano when I was six. I hated it but I got pretty good. They finally let me quit at age ten and I never played again. I started on guitar at age fourteen, just as something to do after school. I never thought it would become my life and career.

How did you first come to hear Jerry Garcia's and/or the Grateful Dead's music? Were you a fan when you first heard it?

I was always interested in music as a kid and I had my own little collection of albums on cassette, but I didn't really get into rock and roll until I started playing guitar at the age of fourteen. All of a sudden I was hearing Jimi Hendrix, Led Zeppelin, the Allman Brothers and Eric Clapton, as if for the first time, and I ate it all up. I got into almost every classic rock band other than the Dead. Some friends tried to turn me on to them but they didn't draw me in at first for some reason. I didn't come back around to it until I started to smoke cannabis and especially after I tried LSD for the first time. Then the music made sense, especially the early psychedelic stuff. The album *Aoxomoxoa* really gave my head a spin once I discovered psychedelics. It may seem like this panders to stereotypes of the Dead being a drug band and Deadheads being druggies, but those of us who have studied the history of the band understand how big a role the psychedelic experience had on the formation of the music and the band as a group mind, so it makes sense in an analytical way. I don't have to be stoned to listen to the Dead or enjoy a concert, but that catalyst helped me to understand the music. From the moment I made that discovery for myself, I ate up all the live tapes and studio albums of the Grateful Dead and Jerry Garcia Band that I could. I was obsessed with the music throughout my late teens. I caught eighteen Grateful Dead shows and two Jerry Garcia Band shows before Jerry died in 1995. I was nineteen at the time and just as lost as many of the other Deadheads. Thank god I had my own musical path to pursue.

(Tyler Grant digs in under the hot lights. Photo by David Tracer.)

When did you start playing out?

I'd become a good guitar player and was studying music at Grossmont College when I joined the Electric Waste Band, who are now in their thirty-fifth year of a Monday night residency at Winston's in Ocean Beach (San Diego). I played Grateful Dead and JGB covers with them every Monday from 1996 to 1998, when I transferred to CalArts in Santa Clarita to complete my bachelor's in music performance. I cut my teeth as a performer, singer and guitarist on that gig, and learned all the songs and Jerry guitar parts. I didn't transcribe a lot of solos or licks from Jerry. The music was so ingrained in my psyche that I didn't need to. It all flowed out naturally. I felt like I could channel the energy and most of the right notes right away with little effort. I got into Jerry's vocal phrasing as well, once I got over trying to sing like Gregg Allman. After graduating CalArts in 2000 I returned to San Diego for a couple years and resumed the Electric Waste Band gig. Then I left for Nashville in 2003 to pursue my music career, which had taken a serious bluegrass turn on a national level.

What was it about Jerry and/or the Grateful Dead that drew you in?

Some of the first Grateful Dead songs I heard, when I was fifteen and a friend tried to turn me on to them, were "Uncle John's Band," "Saint Stephen" and "Truckin'," all from the *Greatest Hits* album. I understood that the songs told stories and had characters, but I just wasn't intrigued enough to get into it. Once I did get into it, around the age of seventeen, with the help of psychedelics, I was captivated by the greater story of the band and how the sound had evolved over the years. There was so much interesting sonic material to dig into. I also got into the songs and stories. As a songwriter and a student of music, that part of it has been a lot more significant in my adulthood, beginning around the time I started recognizing the power of mythology, archetypes and references drawn from the collective unconscious. I witnessed some great performances by Garcia and the Grateful Dead, and I also witnessed the painful decline of Garcia in 1994-1995.

When was your first Dead show?

The first show I attended was December 10, 1993, at the San Diego Sports Arena. I was pretty well-studied on the music by then, and this was their first San Diego appearance in years following a ban from the city. I saw both shows of that run and they were fantastic. I had no idea what to expect when I drove into the parking lot. I witnessed the moving city of Deadheads there, Shakedown Street, and all that.

Does your flatpicking background serve you when playing Grateful Dead music?

Being a Deadhead certainly helped influence my love of bluegrass and my connection to great flatpicking. Early on in my guitar practice, before I became a "real" bluegrass musician, the Garcia acoustic stuff was accessible and I played some of it. I credit David Gans for turning me on to two bands that would bust the door open for me: Old & In The Way and the David Grisman Quintet (DGQ). I had bluegrass in my blood as it turned out. As a teenage Deadhead guitar player, I thought that the JGAB (Jerry Garcia Acoustic Band) represented bluegrass music, until I heard Old & In The Way doing "Uncle Pen" on the Grateful Dead Hour one night. It was like a light bulb over my head, and I realized, "Bill Monroe! This is what bluegrass is!" I dug through my dad's records and CDs and realized I had listened to a lot of bluegrass and that I loved it. Then one night on the Grateful Dead Hour I heard an instrumental that was obviously David Grisman on mandolin, but definitely NOT Jerry Garcia on acoustic guitar. It was too sophisticated and clean. Come to find out the tune was "Neon Tetra" from DGQ's *Hot Dawg* album, with Tony Rice on guitar. Tony was influenced by Clarence White, and Jerry was a huge fan of Clarence, though he never really got to that level as a flatpicker. Jerry went for five-string banjo instead. Tony was also the original guitarist for the DGQ, and lived in the Bay Area for some time while working with David. So it was all connected. I started with the Garcia acoustic stuff, then expanded to study players like Tony Rice and Clarence White when I got serious about bluegrass flatpicking. And, of course, I dug into traditional bluegrass from Bill Monroe, Flatt & Scruggs, the Stanley Brothers and the rest of the first- and second-generation of bluegrass music, which is what Garcia had cut his teeth on as a banjo player.

What kind of guitars do you favor and do you have a specific guitar or effects pedal that you like to use when you're going for the Jerry tone?

On acoustic guitar, it's the same as the flatpicking setup. A nice Martin or Martin-style dreadnought with a flatpick, playing loud with big tone. On electric guitar, the main component is the amp and speakers. I play more of a classic Strat-style Jerry setup, like *Europe '72* era. The JBL speakers in the Twin Reverb just kinda give you that big, bright, fat low-end, Jerry tone. Other than that, I use a delay pedal sometimes when the music calls for a pretty or spacey sound.

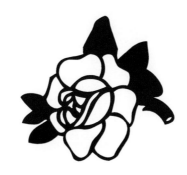

(Joe Craven. Placerville, CA. 2019. Photo by Hal Masonberg.)

Joe Craven

J oe Craven brings welcome doses of whimsicality and virtuosity to his music. Which is probably why Jerry Garcia chose him to be part of the Grammy-nominated Garcia-Grisman project in 1991. Craven is a musical omnivore and his passion for a variety of genres bubbles through whether he's diving into Gypsy Jazz or reinventing a Grateful Dead classic such as "Friend of the Devil." Craven defies musical boundaries and likes it.

How did you first come to hear Jerry Garcia's and/or the Grateful Dead's music?

While in high school in Atlanta, I was listening to records at Peter Buck's (guitarist of REM) house one afternoon. Peter and I occasionally played music together in rag-tag garage bands back then. He put on the newly released *Mars Hotel* (1974) and that was my introduction to the Dead. Soon after that I heard the record *Old & In The Way* (1975). That was the year I graduated high school. From there, Peter became a founding member of REM and I took a mandolin off to college in South Carolina.

Were you a fan when you first heard the music?

I did not connect with the Dead's sound right off. Old & In The Way, however, really made an impression on me, especially Jerry's banjo syncopations and the innovative and brilliant fiddling of Vassar Clements. So my first real connection to Jerry was his banjo playing rather than his beloved guitar playing. In college, I bungee-jumped from progressive string band music or what became known as "New Acoustic Music" (Tony Trischka, Russ Barenberg, Andy Statman and, of course, the David Grisman Quintet), to jazz fusion (late period Miles, Weather Report, Oregon, Jean Luc-Ponty, Alan Holdsworth, etc.). It wasn't until post-college when I moved to Nevada that I heard a Dead recording that caught my ear and interest: *Terrapin Station*. It was different.

What were some of your early influences?

The records my parents put on our old Zenith stereo in the sixties were probably my first influences – Henry Mancini, The Tijuana Brass, The New Christy Minstrels, Andy Williams. My sister Cyndi took an interest in music before me and her love of folk music influenced me as well, from James Taylor to the Monroe-inspired bluegrass of High Country.

Is there any kind of music you don't like?

As I like to say, "I love country music… I don't care what country it comes from!" I tend to follow a leave-no-genre-behind policy of music enjoyment.

What was it about Jerry that you liked?

Jerry will always be an enigma; Robert Hunter referred to it as "the essential mystery" of Jerry. He was intelligent, well-read and complicated. I'm intrigued by artists who live complicated lives. There were also the very private and unassuming sides to Jerry. Yet I had more than a few occasions to speak with him alone in mutual interest and enthusiasm which I'll always cherish. What I knew of him before and after our time together, was actually all within the time I spent with him in the recording studio at David Grisman's house in Mill Valley and the backstages of the original Sweetwater Saloon, The Warfield Theater and at Squaw Valley. At the time, I didn't really get how highly revered he was by so many people. He always made me feel comfortable around him, though, and I appreciated that. Of course, I would not have been there if I had not been recommended and auditioned for the gig by David Grisman, which I'm grateful to David for.

Were you ever a "Deadhead" and, if so, how many shows did you take in?

I did not grow up as a Deadhead. I saw only one show and only because I was in the David Grisman Quintet at that time. It was when we opened for the Grateful Dead at Cal Expo.

What did you think of the Grateful Dead "scene?"

I think that depends on how you define "scene." It's an artful-living brand with its own look, sound and smell. It's a lifestyle, a culture, an affirmation, a spirituality and a beacon. It's bedrock and enhancement, and it will balance your checkbook while doing your windows. It is truly tribal. It has grown into a global mega-community of peaceful unity born out of people's attraction to an alternative perspective. Now it surrounds, inspires and nurtures what has become an entire genre of music known as "jamband."

Can you remember a colorful story from your Jerry history?

Here's an image for you to contemplate. My son, a toddler in diapers, backstage at the Warfield Theater, sitting across the table and eating dinner - alone - with Jerry.

Do you think the music of Jerry and the Dead has changed at all since Garcia passed?

Yes. Creative expression by its very nature, creates uniqueness every time it happens. An interesting irony, however, is when people allow themselves to get caught up in the "correctness" of things and the nostalgia – to relive rather than live anew through art engagement and expression. If something "drifts too far from the shore," it can make folks uncomfortable at times. It's perhaps the concern that something they love could be lost if it's not in the same cubby hole that they can always go to. Like jazz itself, the music of the Grateful Dead can create a dichotomy of tradition versus innovation that folks may have to wrestle with at times.

Are there any particular artists who cover and/or interpret the Dead who you particularly enjoy?

I'd like to answer the question this way . . . I'd love to hear how artists like Tom Waits, Bill Frisell, Ry Cooder, Joni Mitchell, Wynton Marsalis, The Horseflies, Mark Knopfler, The Punch Brothers, Dolly Parton, John Zorn, Molly Tuttle . . . and The San Francisco Philharmonic would cover Grateful Dead music. I'd love to hear artists from other parts of the world weighing in—from the West African, Caribbean, Asian, Arabic and Eastern European traditions.

How do you feel about the proliferation of Dead music?

In terms of its tremendous success in drawing people together on common ground, regardless of their differences, the music of the Dead has been a blessing. Considering its huge popularity and the culture it has spawned, I tend to think it's a good thing.

What kind of instruments do you favor, and what effects or pedals, if any, do you use when playing in the Garcia style?

I favor the use of any instruments in the music. I'm a percussionist and a fiddle and mandolin player and I like them all in the music I recorded and played with Jerry in the Garcia-Grisman band and in my own interpretations as a band leader with my group Joe Craven & The Sometimers. As the percussionist and fiddler for the David Grisman Quintet during the Garcia-Grisman years, it was a natural thing to bring the same tool box I used in David's group to Jerry and David's quartet.

Any other thoughts about Jerry and his musical legacy?

When you're proclaimed a music innovator, whether you're deliberate in your actions towards that or not, you wind up presenting the perfect wrong note. Wrong in that's it's new… new in its placement and new in its timbre. It's different, perhaps strange … and it helps us feel and see the world differently. Jerry Garcia did that.

(Marcus Rezak. Shred is Dead. 2019. Photo courtesy of Ali Jay.)

Marcus Rezak

W hen we spoke, Marcus Rezak was in the process of picking up an "old speaker from the Wall of Sound" for his stage rig. At thirty-six, Rezak says he regretfully never made it to a Grateful Dead show, but that it hasn't stopped him from chasing the magic that he wasn't able to experience first-hand. His band, Shred is Dead, which features a revolving door of talented players from different regions, aims to take the music of Jerry and company to bolder new places, while still honoring the sound that originally served as Rezak's inspiration.

Where are you from?

I was Born and raised in Chicago and then I went to Berklee College of Music in Boston. I loved it there. After graduating I moved back to Chicago. I performed and toured out of Chicago for many years before moving out to Los Angeles. I went to California to expand my horizons. I got to play with a lot of cool musicians there, including some people from Frank Zappa's band and from David Bowie's band. Last year I moved to the Denver area. I'm stationed out of Broomfield, Colorado, now.

So how'd you find your way to Dead World?

I guess it started out with my uncle who was a Deadhead who sang and played guitar when I was a baby. Then later when I was ten years old at camp this one guy had a Rosebud logo hat and I asked him about it. He told me all about the Grateful Dead. The name just grabbled me right away. I was really interested by it all and he gave me *American Beauty* to listen to and it grew from there. Around that time I found my uncle's old guitars at my grandparents' house and everything just took off from there. Eventually I started taking lessons from a Deadhead guitar instructor and it became all I wanted to do when I was in high school. I was the hippie musician who would entertain my classmates with those songs. I studied jazz and stuff at Berklee but it's all come around full circle and now I'm back to playing Dead. It never left me. The musical aesthetic of albums like *Europe '72* and *Reckoning* made a lasting impact.

Was there a particular Dead song that really hit you when you were starting out?

"Jack Straw" from *Europe '72*. It spoke to me. It just sounded beautiful the way they played it. Jerry always outlined the chords' shapes, added chromaticism and bent the notes strikingly.

Did you ever get to any live Grateful Dead performances?

Sadly, no. The closest I ever got was the Fare Thee Well shows in 2015. I attended Furthur Festival when I was young. And a bunch of Phil & Friends and RatDog shows, which I loved. But the Fare Thee Well shows were the closest I've come to what the original thing must have been like. The energy of that experience was not like anything else I'd experienced before.

What's behind your band name Shred is Dead?

It's related to the shredding aspect of the guitar and the way we interpret the music. I like to take the Grateful Dead and make it a little more high octane, a little faster, a little more energized. That's the way I like to play it, which is kind of an evolution from some of the jazz and bluegrass projects that spun off the Dead, including projects like Jazz is Dead, which I like a lot. It's about having a certain edge to it and a little more of a progressive-y glisten.

(Marcus Rezak. Photo by David Tracer)

Does Shred is Dead feature a stable lineup?

I bring in different people. It depends on the region where I'm playing and who is available. Each lineup keeps getting better. I just played in Vermont with Russ Lawton from Trey Anastasio's band on drums and the bass player Zdenek Gubb from Twiddle and a guy named Scott Hannay on keys. I've played with people like Jay Lane and Reid Mathis and that was really fun. I've also played with David Gans. Just really great musicians. I like to try and spread the love around and keep it exciting for myself too. It's fun to see where the music can go with the different chemistries. I sort of have an outline that we can color in or go outside of. I try to keep it consistent while always adding new people into the mix. I'm the core person and I try to build these lineups and work around their other bands. I like to have a good vibe and carry on the tradition of the music in the right way. Not all of the players come from the Grateful Dead world and that creates uniqueness. It can get really interesting.

Do you have a fixed approach to your shows?

I try to have a planned setlist, but audibles get called. I like to keep it organic and in-the-moment, but it's nice to have a general outline to go from. I'll get into my zone and neurons start firing off my brain about what should happen and I just let it hit me. I've played one song for an entire set before, just exploring it. We'll play stuff by other musicians too, not just the Dead. Mostly sixties- and seventies-era rock. Stuff by the Allman Brothers, Bob Dylan, Eric Clapton, Jimi Hendrix and Janis Joplin. I want to be part of the next generation of Dead players who bring the music into the present time and space. We do unique arrangements but we still do traditional versions of songs too. Things you don't want to change because they're so perfect, like "Black Muddy River." But then we also do instrumental versions of "Scarlet Begonias," "Dark Star," "Unbroken Chain," "King Solomon's Marbles," "Liberty" and "Broken Arrow." I do a very unique arrangement of "Estimated Prophet" with a steppers reggae vibe. People always ask for that one.

How do you feel about all this playing Dead?

Some of it is sort of funny and some of it's great. It can be a little too done or main-brand at times, with people doing it just because it's cool. Whereas other people play it because they've been fans for a long time. It's all over the place. But I think that the music deserves to be heard by lots of people and hopefully it influences them in positive ways and helps make society better.

How do people respond to your version of this music?

Everyone seems to really like the uniqueness, the freshness and the dance-party vibe and edge. It's different. We get a diverse audience. I feel really good about the response. We're getting good love from people. I just want to keep playing for more people and spreading the word.

What do you use in terms of gear to get your Jerry tone?

Well the speaker is the main source of my tone. It's a JBL E120 that I got from an old Deadhead in San Francisco. On the inside there's a little sticker that reads "Wall." It's very transparent and clean and just sounds really good. Then I use a classic old Fender Twin amp head that runs to a speaker cabinet. I use all classic fifties and sixties tubes in the amp head. Having nice tubes really helps. I use a Mike Beigel Mu-FX Tru-Tron envelope filter, which is similar to a Mu-Tron. It's the bigger white one, not the little blue one. It kicks ass. I use it in conjunction with the black Digitech WhammyII pedal that Trey Anastasio kind of popularized and which produces a thick octave. The two of those pedals together really nail the auto-wah and octave sound that Jerry coined. And I use some other pedals that aren't really Jerry related but that I like. The rest is all in my fingers. I have a Mike Lippe USA guitar. I love it. Tone can be about ninety percent in your fingers. You get the sound in your ear and then you have to reproduce it with your hands. I get good feedback about my tone, so I figure I'm doing something right.

Anything else you want to add about Jerry?

Jerry masterfully played his guitar, but his personality was great too. Just his presence was great. That can be really important. It affects people. His voice contained passion and honesty and he sang from the soul.

(Joe Marcinek finding Jerry's intention. Photo by Libby Gamble.)

Joe Marcinek

Next-gen Dead jammer Joe Marcinek started out as the keyboardist for Terrapin Flyer before picking up a six-string and taking his act on the road with a revolving lineup of players all across the country. The thirty-four-year-old Marcinek takes a refreshingly big-picture approach to Jerry's music while sharing his creative joy with musicians of all walks.

Can you share your music origin story and how you came to be part of the world of the Dead?

When I was growing up I had a buddy who played acoustic guitar. We used to hang around in the basement of his house and I thought it was really cool that he could play some of the songs that we heard on the radio. I remember wanting to learn how to play and in October of 2000 he sold me one of his Samick acoustics and that's when I picked it up. I was never good at sports or anything so I took right to the world of music. I started out with some classic rock stuff that I was into at the time and then I discovered Phish and Widespread Panic and the Grateful Dead as I got further into high school. When it was time to go to college I decided to pursue music as a career. I'd gotten an A+ in music theory my senior year in high school, so I decided to study it in college too, for a couple years, and then I also studied the business side of music. I figured that might be more practical.

After graduating from college, I joined a couple bands and played around Chicago. I got the opportunity to join Doug Hagman and Terrapin Flyer in 2013 as the band's keyboardist. I was lucky to play with them on a weekly basis for about two years. I wasn't a hardcore Deadhead when I started with them but it allowed me to grow a true appreciation for the music and the whole scene. On one of those nights it hit me just how cool it was and I caught the bug. We studied whole albums and whole shows. We dug deep into the catalog. When I started playing the songs on the guitar I was familiar with the music from playing it on the keys but I wasn't hung up about doing exactly what Garcia did. There's something abut Grateful Dead tribute music on the guitar where everyone is completely obsessed with what Jerry did. I was lucky because I learned the music on a keyboard, so I wasn't tied up in trying to copy his style. I was able to be more free. When I started playing the music on the guitar I just wanted to emulate his intention. I was looking more to get into the spirit of it and connect with the energy that he put out. When you come to hear me play that should comes across.

But you know some of Jerry's licks right?

Oh yeah, it's almost like telling old stories. There are certain key points, or signature licks in this case, that make it that particular story, and over the years everyone puts their own spin on it. You try to personalize the story. In a song such as "Scarlet Begonias," you're going to play the signature notes, but when

you go to the improv section that's where you use your own voice. I play with different lineups all over the country. I've played with hundreds of players now. I've been working with Melvin Seals recently. He played with Jerry a lot. You can see when you play with Melvin why Jerry loved playing with him. Because Melvin is such a responsive player.

Do you like some of the next-generation artists who play Dead?

Yeah, I've worked a bit with Holly Bowling and Tom Hamilton from Ghost Light. They're amazing. Holly does solo piano versions of Grateful Dead songs that are super cool and Tom also plays in JRAD.

Are there any special songs from the catalog that really speak to you?

I try to keep it open and it's always evolving over time. The first song I really got into was "I Know You Rider" from *Europe '72*, which is one of my favorite albums of all time. Then I got into songs like "Estimated Prophet," "Help On the Way," "Terrapin Station," and "Dark Star." I definitely have some go-to songs that I like to play. It's hard to pick your favorites. I love Jerry's version of "Knockin' on Heavens Door." There's so much to dig into.

Any last thoughts about Garcia?

At music school I was exposed to a lot of stuff including world, jazz and classical, but I also love punk, acoustic and bluegrass. So I have some parallels with Garcia in terms of that. Jerry wasn't just into one kind of music. I think that's why his music brings together so many different people with different backgrounds. There's so much influence there.

(Adam Perry. Photo by Gwendolyn Anne Ross.)

Adam Perry

Drummer and music journalist Adam Perry isn't a typical Deadhead, if you could call him a Deadhead at all, though he has played and continues to play with people in the Grateful Dead music scene on occasion. When he's not jamming with some of Jerry's kids, Perry also plays with the alt-folk rock group The Gasoline Lollipops out of Boulder, Colorado.

How'd you first get into playing and how'd you end up brushing up against the music of Jerry and the Dead?

I grew up in Pittsburgh, where I began playing the drums when I was nine. Starting in fifth grade I was in punk bands and from the time I was fifteen or sixteen I was playing in clubs and bars. I was anti-hippie and anti-Grateful Dead growing up. I remember the last time the Dead played in Pittsburgh in 1995 a friend of mine said "I'll buy you a ticket you should go see this!" I was like "Fuck that, that's stupid." But eventually I came to be friends with the writer [and longtime Deadhead] Steve Silberman in college and he got me into them when I was about twenty-one and I started listening to their tapes. When I moved out to the San Francisco Bay Area I started playing music with people including Robyn Sylvester, Rob Barraco, Jay Lane and Mark Karan who are really amazing musicians and who are associated with that scene. I don't really listen to the Dead's music anymore although I will every now and then. There's definitely some good stuff out there.

What's your take on musicians who take their cues from the Dead these days?

I think it's most interesting when people pay tribute to Jerry and the Dead in a way that's unique. I don't like it when musicians just regurgitate something or follow a blueprint that was created by someone else. The Dead were actually one of the first indie bands, they literally had an indie label. So you can also be influenced by the way the band approached the music business. I like the way that the group The National was influenced by the Dead. I think that Jerry Garcia in particular would be way more interested in bands that liked his music and then went on to do something new with that influence. You can love the Dead but you don't have to sound like them. I don't think Jerry would give a shit about some of the bands that just imitate his style. The music of the Grateful Dead actually has a lot of darkness to it. A song like "Black Peter" is really dark. I think that most jambands in general are lacking in anything dark or edgy which is why I find them boring. I think Jerry would too. Jerry was influenced by music with darker themes, including stuff by the Carter Family.

129

When you play Dead music how do you approach it as a drummer?

It's less about execution and practice and more about stretching things out and getting into a groove. In the jamband world there isn't a lot of rehearsal. Everyone knows the songs so you get together to have fun and see what happens. That's kind of the mentality. In general I'm not really interested in seeing musicians just jamming unless it's a jazz band. There's usually one guy up there soloing who is a virtuoso and you're laying down a groove for them. There are definitely some amazing guitarists on the jam scene though, such as Derek Trucks and Jimmy Herring who can take it out there on their solos and who also write good music, though a lot of it just seems like people noodling.

Do you enjoy it when you play Dead?

The shows I've played with people like David Gans, Barry Sless and David Nelson have been great. I don't play this music all the time so it makes it more exciting when I do. Later in life I started liking Bill Kreutzmann's drumming a lot, especially during the phase when he was the only drummer for the Grateful Dead. The Dead were amazing and the reason they have a legacy is that they were music geeks who listened to a lot of weird stuff. The release *Day of the Dead* (2016) is a good example of indie bands doing interesting stuff with that influence. I mean check out the Dead's first album [from 1967], the fast one [*The Grateful Dead*]. Imagine if that was the only album they ever made? And then they got really weird and experimental on their second release *Anthem of the Sun* (1968). I think that Jerry would be proud if someone made something incredibly weird and original. That's what the Grateful Dead means to me. Because life includes happiness, darkness and all the stuff in between.

(Josh Olken, far right, and Terrapin Flyer. Photo by Liz Gleeson.)

Josh Olken

Thirty-one-year-old Josh Olken is a member of the Chicago-based Grateful Dead- and JGB-inspired tribute band Terrapin Flyer. The group often features original Jerry Garcia Band member Melvin Seals on keys and over the years has taken in a host of different musicians. Olken, who is schooled in jazz, performs astoundingly authentic-sounding guitar solos in the style of Garcia. The skilled Chicagoan wows audiences across the country as he and the members of Flyer dive into spirited versions of material from the Dead and JGB catalogs.

How long have you been playing with Terrapin Flyer?

Uh, let's see. I started around 2014. I was kind of the local guy for a bit and then I began touring around with [Terrapin Flyer] and Melvin in 2015. I've been blessed to do about seventy or something shows with Melvin since then.

Did you study jazz formally?

Yeah, after graduating from high school I went to the School For Jazz and Contemporary Music at The New School in New York City, where I studied improvised music and free jazz and stuff like that.

Did you like New York?

Yeah, it was a great time to be there because Phil and Bobby were pretty obsessed with New York and they played a lot while I was going to school there. I got to take in a bunch of shows as part of the *Philathon* runs at the Nokia Theater at Times Square [2007-2008]. They did a fourteen-night stretch one of those years. So I never got to see Jerry but I got to see a whole lot of Phil.

Well, you've obviously done some serious listening to Jerry based on what I've heard from your playing?

Yeah, I don't even want to know how many hours I've put into listening to the Dead and Jerry-related music. I get totally immersive. That's how to really get into it. When you listen to it that much it just gets in your bones.

Do you try to replicate the sound of certain eras? I watched a version of "Eyes of the World" on YouTube that you did with Melvin Seals and it was incredibly authentic sounding, a lot like the great seventies versions . . .

It depends. Sometimes we'll try and set a theme or cop a certain vibe. I do remember talking to one of my bandmates about some of the stuff I'd been listening to the day of the show. We were tapping into some slightly faster version of "Eyes." In general, with Jerry, I feel like there are some set parameters with the vocabulary and then within those parameters you can express your individuality. I have some favorite years. It just depends on the day.

(Melvin Seals keeps the flame alive and inspires new players. Rich Saputo.)

I saw Melvin was smiling and he looked like he was enjoying what you were playing . . .

Yeah, we have a cool repertoire together. We end up trading licks. Doug [Hagman], who runs Terrapin Flyer, said "Wow, Melvin doesn't usually do that with anyone." It's definitely trippy to look up and see Melvin there. It's like, "Whoa." But we'll trade solos on tunes like "Don't Let Go" and "West L.A. Fadeaway" and "The Way you Do the Things you Do." I let Melvin start it. I don't force it. He's the king. We've also played with [keyboardists] including Scott Guberman and Tom Constanten who are a lot of fun to jam with.

So do you have an overall approach to playing Jerry?

I find with this music that it's a lot like jazz, which is what I studied and what helped prepare me for live performance. But yeah, Jerry was really tapped into playing the changes and having pretty logical phrases where he outlined the chords. He would start and end on a guide tone, which I try to do too. I craft my lines to create melodies. Some of the things I've learned from Melvin include how to build a solo dynamically. It's a whole experience, where you create a story with different motifs and then blend them. In the book *Jerry on Jerry* [by Dennis McNally] Jerry talks about the Jack Kerouac style of writing where Kerouac used a continuous roll of paper so he could just keep typing and get his ideas out spontaneously. Jerry came from that beatnik ethos and I try and apply that musically. I like to come up with slightly different licks and interweave them creatively. It depends on the tune too. Playing Grateful Dead and Jerry Garcia Band requires different approaches. JGB is more of a down-home and traditional feel. If we're covering both bands in one set, it will take you for a little trip.

How do you feel about so many people playing this music these days?

My take is that it's kind of like how jazz guys back in the day played. It used to be Cole Porter songs or George Gershwin tunes or the standards in the song book. The Hunter-Garcia book is the new vernacular. The song forms are so open to individuality and interpretation that you have something for everybody. For the kid who's into noise music like the '68 Grateful Dead sound, or whatever, you can find something for anyone. You've got the purists and also the people who like to try and do different things with it. I think this music's going to last forever. It blows my mind. It's just so strong.

Olken Gear

I run a McIntosh MC-2100 through a Sarno preamp with a Wald-Electronics Spud buffer and I use JBL speakers. I've got a Mu-FX Tru-Tron 3x envelope filter and a Mu-FX octave divider (both by Mike Beigel). For guitar, I usually use a Carvin DC400, which was modded by Brian White. But lately I've been using a Tiger replica by Moriarty Guitars. My tech gave it to me. The cool thing about it is the middle pickup. We got it from a Steve Parish sale on Ebay. It's one of Jerry's pickups that they used as a backup for the Tiger from '83 to '87. I use a Boss DD7 as a delay. A lot of what I do depends on the night and what sound I'm trying to cop.

All interviews in *Channeling Jerry* were done by Nick Hutchinson and took place between the summer of 2019 and the spring of 2020.

ABOUT THE AUTHOR

A fan of the music of the Grateful Dead since the early eighties, Nick Hutchinson has played in a few Dead cover bands. He attended his first live Grateful Dead show at the Saratoga Performing Arts Center in Saratoga Springs, NY, in 1984, and experienced many live performances by the Grateful Dead and the Jerry Garcia Band until 1995 when Jerry played his last song. Nick works as a freelance writer and editor. He and his family live in Denver.

Backers

Channeling Jerry would not have come into being without the support and generosity of the people who contributed to the project through GoFundMe. My sincere thanks goes out to the following donors:

Richard Baldwin
Tim Billings
John Britton
Posey Cochrane
Peter Collins
Jeff Delaney
Nate Downey
Jeff Eldridge
Court Fawcett
Patrick Flood
David Foulke
John Greene
Walter Hajduk
Paul and Jacqueline Hutchinson
Dennis McNally
William Maeck
Terry Martin
Ted Maynard
Alexandra Strawbridge-Maurer
Fairfax O'Riley
Nick Paumgarten
Dylan Ray

Olivia Ray

Diane and Paul Reilly

Marc Robert

Kim Scheinberg

Keith Steiduhar

Anne and Robert Sacks

Jocelyn and David Sand

Charlie Shaffer

Tony Stack

Liza Vergez

Mark Vossler

August West

Chris Wirth

James Young